AF333998

The Book of
POTIONS

Follow the Gastronogeek authors on their adventures
at www.gastronogeek.com
and facebook.com/gastronogeek

Thibaud **VILLANOVA**

Stéphanie **SIMBO**

The Book of POTIONS

PHOTOGRAPHS
Guillaume **CZERW**

STYLING
Sophie **DUPUIS-GAULIER**

EDITORIAL PACKAGING
Le **BDAG**

ILLUSTRATIONS
Bérengère **DEMONCY**

TITAN
BOOKS

It's been over a year since I took the helm of what Chef Thierry Marx kindly dubbed "the *Gastronogeek* ship". We've come a long way since we launched our first book and embarked on this journey!

Gastronogeek serves as a bridge between imagination and cuisine—be it grand or homemade, street food or grandma's cooking—all while emphasizing healthiness and respect for seasons, products, and proper culinary techniques. My encounters with chefs, artisans, producers, brewers, and catering professionals, coupled with my immersion in imaginary cultures, have inspired me to create a medium bridging generations. In doing so, this unites geeks and non-geeks of the past and present, while paving the way for the enthusiasts of tomorrow. I aim to demonstrate that being a geek in the kitchen doesn't mandate a diet solely of chips, pizzas, and sodas while watching movies or TV series. I acknowledge and respect everyone's choices in how they eat and live.

To me, *Gastronogeek* embodies its universe. It's both a bustling restaurant kitchen and the laboratory of a star cruiser. It's a pantry meticulously curated by a hobbit moments before dinner, disrupted by 12 dwarves and a wizard. It's an alchemical cabinet adorned with vials and containers. It's a dimly-lit room illuminated by candles or a crackling hearth, simmering with sweet-smelling potions.

Above all, geek culture and gastronomy revolve around pleasure, emotions, and traditions. Through my books, I strive to contribute a small piece to this vast edifice—that's my credo.

And today, thanks to you, dear reader, I present a second volume: Gastronogeek, the Book of Potions. For this book, I've collaborated with Stéphanie Simbo, a young barmaid, alchemist, and mixologist from London. Her creativity, energy, and enthusiasm have enriched our team, presenting her alcoholic creations for this occasion! Together, we offer you a guide to gastronomy and mixology. This time, explore recipes for soups, smoothies, sauces, and cocktails inspired by the references covered in the first volume, alongside over 40 carefully selected new references, including a chapter dedicated to video games.

Discover the crafting of Romulan ale, the same drink McCoy offered Kirk when he was a Starfleet admiral! Taste an asparagus cream as made in Cardinal de Richelieu's Paris and relish the spice-infused coffee wisely prepared by the valiant Fremen! Let's unlock the secrets of geek culture's potions together!

To accompany you on this culinary voyage into imaginary cultures, I've added extracts from The Chronicles of the Traveller of Worlds at the end of each chapter. Who is he, you ask? A whimsical and zany adventurer, offering sound advice and recommendations!

As you flip through these pages, discover the ultimate adventure companion…

Happy reading and bon appétit!

Thibaud Villanova

Traditionally, there are only two kinds of cookbooks for us geeks:

1. Those simply adorning basic dishes, often with colored marzipan, resembling our favorite universes—muffins shaped like Mario's mushrooms, Captain America's shield on pancakes, a Pac-Man-shaped pizza, a *Star Wars* Star Destroyer pie slice, eggs decorated with green peas like Yoshi's or onion rings from *The Lord of the Rings* that aren't that "precious".

2. The ones compiling ultra-simple junk food recipes like "Order a 'four ham' pizza named 'Speed-Jabba Hutt,' wait for the moped delivery, and indulge in the oily cardboard box delight!"

Gastronogeek *takes a more nuanced approach, offering real, superb food recipes inspired by the imaginary cultures close to our hearts.*

For these "little guy-stronomes," there's no taking the easy way out, unless for a clever pun like "Mos Eisley's Spatio-Pig" or the delight of seeing Sauron's eye appear in a tartlet. *Gastronogeek*'s recipes demand sophistication, refinement, balance, and, above all… deliciousness! If they decide to create "Princess Leia macaroons" inspired by her iconic hairstyle (did that cross your mind, Thibaud?), it goes beyond mere homage— it's a meticulously crafted macaroon recipe worthy of the finest French macaroon artisans!

This time, they venture into liquids, offering a selection of beverages, cocktails, soups, and smoothies—and once again, they succeed! Unfortunately, the recipe for Asterix's magic potion remains elusive! Yet, we know it involves mistletoe, mead, honey, carrots, a pinch of salt, and strawberries or lobster (depending on your preference)... We will need a DLC on the *Gastronogeek* blog!

Marcus, the nutellivorous gastronaut

A veritable "video game dinosaur", Marcus' 25-year career has seen him contribute to some of the oldest and most prestigious titles in the specialist press, including Micro News, Tilt, and Consoles+. He is also one of the pioneers of video games on television, with programs such as Micro Kid's on France 3, Cyber Flash on Canal+, and above all Level One, the show that made him a household name, on Game One. Today, on the Nolife channel, he hosts the show that's closest to his heart, Chez Marcus, in which he pretends he's virtually welcoming viewers into his home to try out a game under live conditions. He hosts the Game One debate, takes part in the daily news program #TeamG1 and tests games in the Game One Box. He also recounts the history of video games in Retro Game One and in several books. He also launched his comic book career, publishing the sequel to the adventures of his childhood superhero, L'Intrépide, 37 years later with Ankama. His versatile career embodies a rich legacy in gaming and beyond.

SCIENCE-FICTION

STAR TREK
Romulan ale
Rum, whiskey, curaçao, and lemon
20

FIREFLY
Irish Xiong Mao Niao
Lapsang Souchong, rye whiskey and lemon
22

BACK TO THE FUTURE
Lou's chocolate milkshake
Chocolate milkshake with dark chocolate chips
24

FANTASY

KAAMELOTT
Vivacity potion
Or healing potion for ingrown toenails,
I'm not sure…
48

HOOK
Crocodile Island
Gold Strike, lime and mint
50

CONAN
Cimmerian warrior tea
Infusion of hibiscus, ginger and red berries
52

MANGA

ATTACK ON TITAN
Souvenir of Shiganshina
Earl Grey, plum wine and blackcurrant liqueur
74

DRAGON BALL
Kamehakarot
Carrot, orange and ginger smoothie
76

NARUTO
Tonkotsu Ramen
with spinach, eggs
and narutomaki
78

STAR WARS

La Corellia
Whiskey, amber beer and cumin
26

Dagobah root stew
Vegetarian root vegetable stew
28

DUNE

Arrakeen Coffee Special
Cinnamon cappuccino
30

DOCTOR WHO

Sexy Blue Box
Tequila, Parfait Amour and curaçao
32

TERMINATOR

Sarakonor
Gin, absinthe, brandy and cherry liqueur
34

STARGATE

Datta Bydos
Date, mango and almond milk
36

H2G2

Pan Galactic Gargle Blaster
Chartreuse, génépi, Get 27, mint, etc.
38

ALIEN

The Eighth Passenger
Guinness, ginger and jasmine
40

Lexicon
42

Tips
43

The World Traveller Chronicles
44

WILLOW

Meegosh's tonic
Spiced wine
54

THE CARDINAL'S BLADES

Danvert cream
Cream of asparagus in a crust
56

HARRY POTTER

Butterbeer restyled
Lager, cider, butter, vanilla and cinnamon
58

Liquid luck
Potion of gin, orange liqueur and champagne
60

DISCWORLD

Nac Mac Micmac
Cardhu, whiskey cream and amber beer
62

THE LORD OF THE RINGS

Ent draught
Woody infusion, rooibos and Mare gin
64

DUNGEONS & DRAGONS

Dwarf beer from the Forgotten Realms
Warm beer with spices
66

Tips
68

Lexicon
69

The World Traveller Chronicles
70

CANDY CANDY

Strawberry happiness
Strawberry and banana smoothie
80

SAINT SEIYA

Preparing for the sanctuary
Hyoga shot,
Phoenix shot,
Pegasus shot,
Dragon shot,
Shun shot
82 - 83

ONE PIECE

Binks No Saké
Captain Morgan, triple sec, pineapple and passion fruit
86

PRINCESS MONONOKE

Avenging Spirits Broth
Japanese broth, leeks and yuzu
88

CITY HALL

Fly to the Moon
Mojito à la Jules Verne
90

SAILOR MOON

Lunar Sceptre
Egg, campari, grapefruit and tequila
92

BLACK JACK

Honma Special
Tequila, ginseng liqueur and turmeric
94

Lexicon
96

Tips
97

The World Traveller Chronicles
98

FANTASTIC

NIGHT OF THE LIVING DEAD

Braaaaiiiiinnn
Brain Hemorrhage variant
102

CTHULHU MYTHOS

Deep Smoked
Fumet of langoustine and saffron chantilly
104

THE GOONIES

Chunkshake
Vanilla milkshake with chocolate and cookie
chips, whipped cream and caramel sauce
106

COMICS

SUPERMAN

Fortress of Solitude
Gin, Get 31 and curaçao
128

BATMAN

The Dark Knight
Eristoff Black vodka, Grey Goose vodka
and dry Noilly Prat
130

Pennyworth's Vichyssoise
Glazed leek and potato soup
132

VIDEO GAMES

FINAL FANTASY

Chocobo Élixir
Eggnog, rum and speculoos
158

FALLOUT

Find the chip!
Ginger beer, white rum and basil
160

THE LEGEND OF ZELDA

The Syrup Witch's potions
Pomegranate juice, vodka and Freixenet;
Fruit mocktail; Spinach and watercress soup;
Inspired by the Blue Lagoon
162

HIGHLANDER

Glenn Finan's twists and turns
Dewar's, Drambuie, Angostura
108

GHOSTBUSTERS

Slimer Jello Shot
Vodka, Get 27 and mint jelly
110

INDIANA JONES

Chachapoyan
Adventure version of Pisco Sour
112

THE ADDAMS FAMILY

The Mamuschka
Chocolate cream, cognac and Licor 43
114

DRACULA

Vin Fiert
Mulled wine with vodka and red fruit
116

BEETLEJUICE

Experiment n°6121
Espresso, White Dog rye whiskey and Tia Maria
118

BIG TROUBLE IN LITTLE CHINA

Shen tonic
Nigori Yuzushu and citrus cocktail
120

Lexicon
122

Tips
123

The World Traveller Chronicles
124

HELLBLAZER

Mucous Membrane
Variation on Snakebite served at Casanova Club in Newcastle
134

HELLBOY

Code Name Red
Bloody Mary revisited
136

THOR

Trio Palatin
Negroni Nordic version
138

GUARDIANS OF THE GALAXY

Galactic Mix
Groooot, Charlie 27, Martinex T'Naga, Starshot, Yondu Udonta
140 - 141

SCOTT PILGRIM

Happy Avocado Vegan Refreshment
Avocado, banana and coconut smoothie
144

DEADPOOL

Comic Awareness
Pulque, mezcal and lime
146

THE HULK

The Mastodon
Cold cucumber, green bell pepper, avocado and piquillo mousse soup
149

Lexicon
150

Tips
152

The World Traveller Chronicles
153

MONKEY ISLAND

Lemonhead
Rum and limoncello
166

SUPER MARIO

Rainbow Road
Vodka, peach liqueur and rainbow ice cubes
168

Chocolate Island
Cocoa gin, Frangelico and crème de cacao
168

POKÉMON

Pokétail
Infused gin, wild strawberries and Campari
170

PRINCE OF PERSIA

Jaffar's Delight
Mint doogh
172

DONKEY KONG

Golden Banana
Banana, Koko Kanu rum and white cocoa
174

ASSASSIN'S CREED

Requiescat in pace
Amaretto, Aperol and gin
177

Lexicon
178

Tips
179

The World Traveller Chronicles
182

E Q U I P M E N T

Electric mixer

Saucepan

Blender

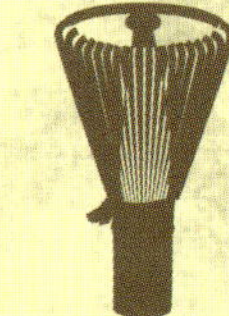

Chasen
(bamboo whisk)

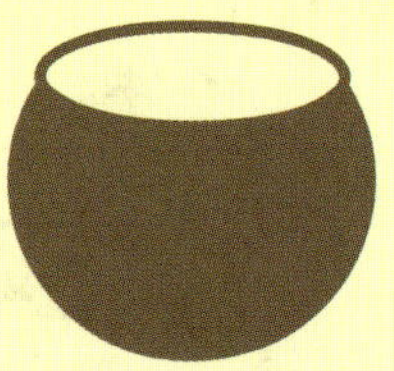

Glass jar

Chawan
(tea bowl)

Bowl

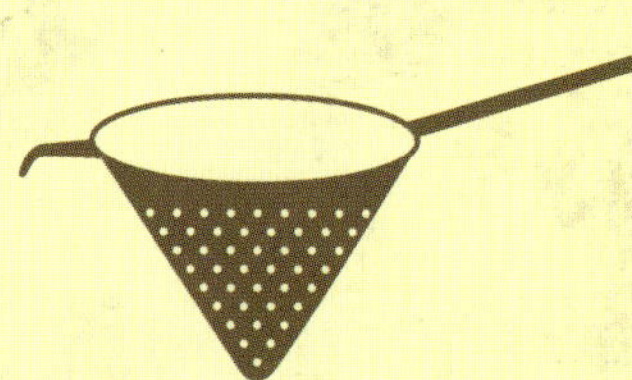

Chinois strainer

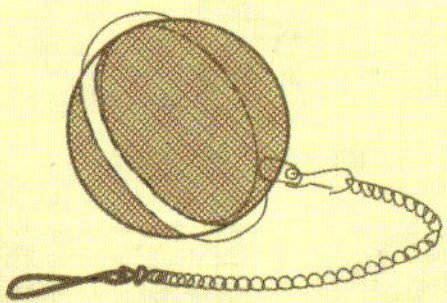

Tea ball

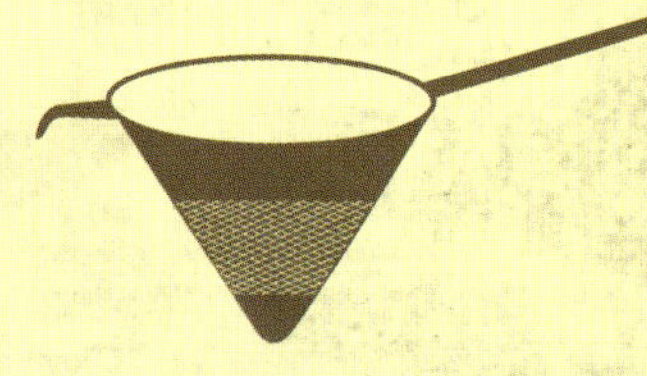

Sieve

Piston coffee maker

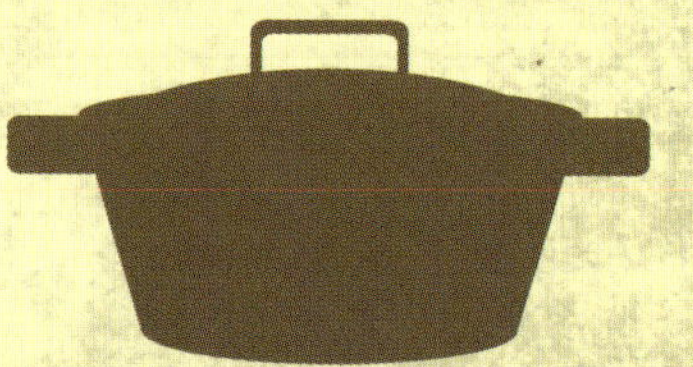

Cast iron casserole dish

Pressure cooker
Skimmer
Ramekin
Paring knife
Dutch oven
Salad bowl
Slicing knife
Whisk
Soup tureen
Fillet of sole knife
Hand blender
Spatula
Coffee spoon
Mixing bowl
Stove
Teapot
Peeler
Pastry bag
Pastry thermometer

ACCESSORIES FOR THE PERFECT BLENDER

Drip tray

Japanese conical bar gauge

Boston shaker

Mortar

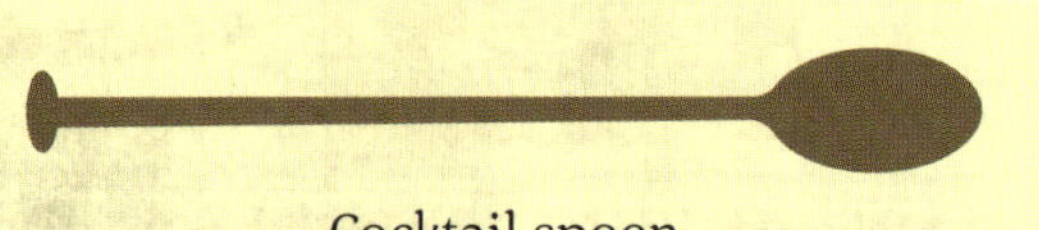

Cocktail spoon

Bottle opener

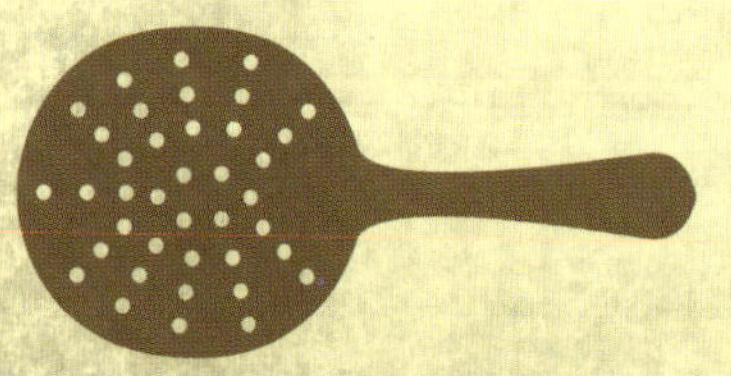

Julep filter

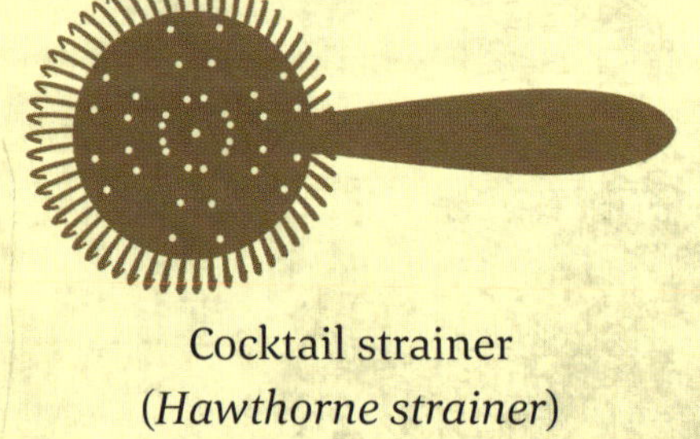

Cocktail strainer
(*Hawthorne strainer*)

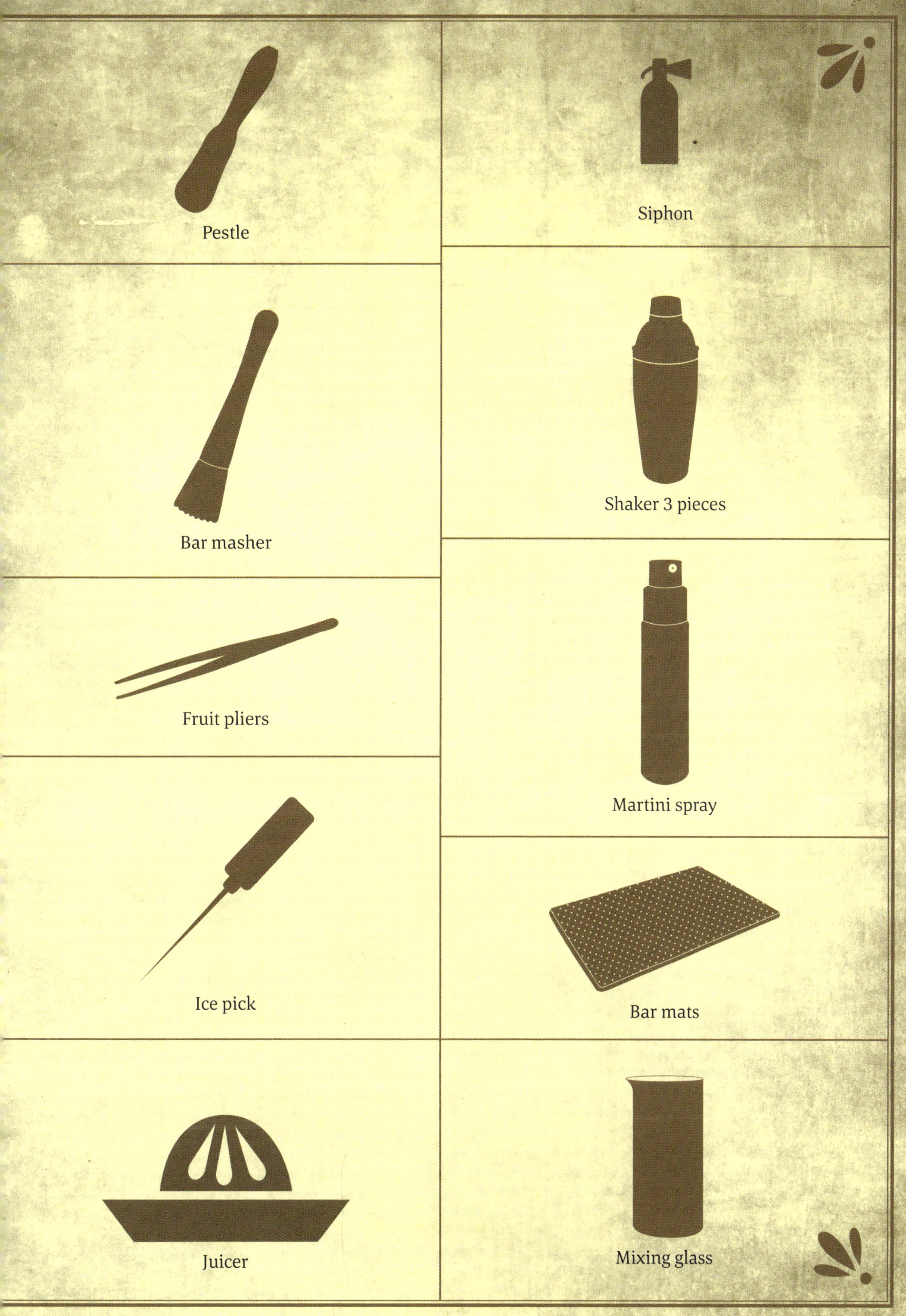

Pestle
Siphon
Bar masher
Shaker 3 pieces
Fruit pliers
Martini spray
Ice pick
Bar mats
Juicer
Mixing glass

GLASSES

Anchovy jar

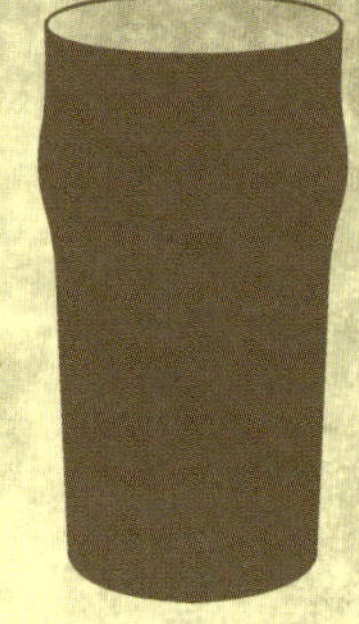

Half

Graal

Beer mug

Potion flask

Laboratory flask

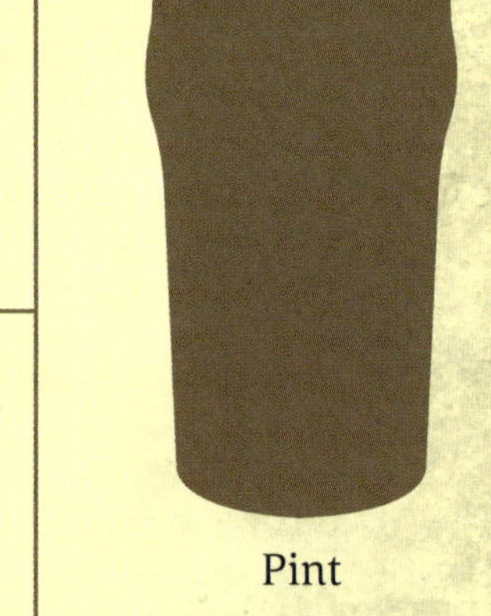

Pint

Cut glass

Metal cutting

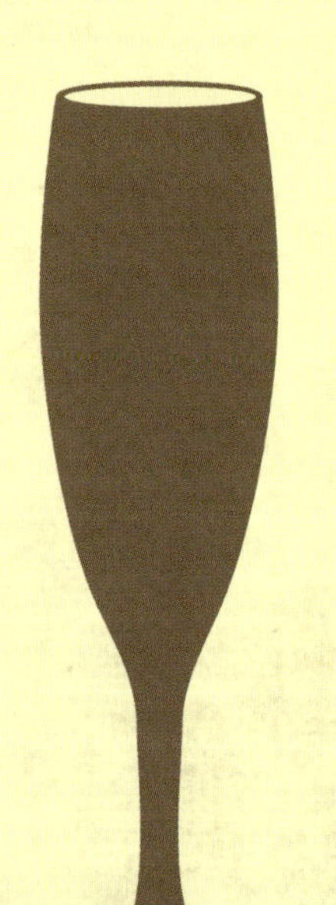

Flute

Old fashioned

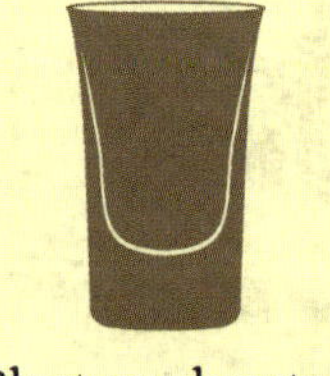

Shot or shooter

Coffee cup

Tea cup
Coffee glass
Smoothie glass
Julep cup
Tumbler
Martini glass
Tea glass
Pilsner glass
Square tumbler
Milkshake glass
Whiskey glass
Pool glass
Tiki
Stemware glass
Balloon glass
Tulip glass

GRAYS
SPORTS
ALM
COMPLET
1950
INCLUDING
BASEBALL, FOOTBALL
BOXING, HORSERACING
AND MORE!

SCIENCE-FICTION

For **1 GLASS** and **A HALF** - Preparation: **5 MIN** - LEVEL ✦ ✦

Here's the kind of drink your doctor friend could have offered you, the kind of drink you could have sipped together while reminiscing about the good old days, those when you travelled throughout the galaxy on behalf of the United Federation of Planets!

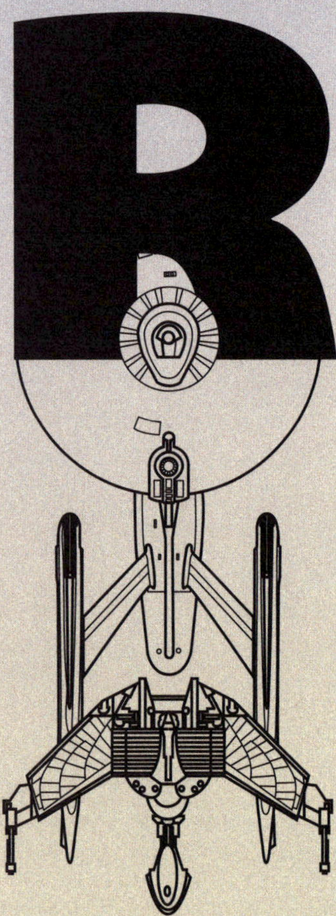

ROMULAN ALE
Rum, whiskey, curaçao and lemon

INGREDIENTS

4 tsp (20 ml) 151 Proof Rum
4 tsp (20 ml) Jameson Irish whiskey
4 tsp (20 ml) curaçao (blue)
2 tsp (10 ml) lemon juice
2 tsp (10 ml) cane sugar
10 tbsp (150 ml) sparkling water
Crushed ice

EQUIPMENT

Boston shaker

For optimal enjoyment of this Romulan ale, ensure to chill the glass by placing it in the freezer for approximately 10 minutes.

Combine the rum, whiskey, curaçao, lemon juice, and cane sugar in a Boston shaker. Add the crushed ice and vigorously shake for about 30 seconds.

Retrieve your glass from the freezer and carefully pour the contents of the shaker into it. Finish by topping up the mixture with sparkling water. Then, savor and enjoy!

For **1 GLASS** - Preparation: **10 MIN** - LEVEL ✦ ✦ ✦

RISH XIONG MAO NIAO
Lapsang Souchong, rye whiskey and lemon

INGREDIENTS

2 ½ tsp (6 g) Lapsang Souchong tea
1 ⅓ cup (300 ml) water
8 tsp (40 ml) Rittenhouse 100 proof rye whiskey
2 tsp (10 ml) lemon juice
20 ml cane sugar syrup
A few slices of ginger
Crushed ice

EQUIPMENT

Teapot
Pastry thermometer
Shaker

Prepare your tea by putting the tea leaves in a teapot strainer. Heat water to 95°C and pour it over the tea. Steep for 4 minutes, then remove the leaves and let the tea cool to room temperature.

Once the tea cools, combine it with whiskey, lemon juice, and cane sugar syrup in a shaker. Add some crushed ice and shake vigorously for 30 seconds.

Pour the shaker's contents into a julep glass, straining out the crushed ice. Discard the used crushed ice and add fresh ice to the shaker. Pour the contents of the julep glass back into the shaker and shake briefly. Return the mixture to the julep glass.

Place ginger slices on the glass rim to infuse the cocktail with flavor. Enjoy your drink!

For 4 MILKSHAKE GLASSES · Preparation: 15 to 30 MIN · LEVEL ✦

If the chocolate milk is a Lou's classic that George McFly likes to order to build up his courage, here's our version of another American diner classic: the milkshake!

OU'S CHOCOLATE MILKSHAKE
Chocolate milkshake with dark chocolate chips

INGREDIENTS

2 cups (500 ml) whipping cream (over 30% fat)
¾ cup (100 g) powdered sugar
2 cups (500 ml) good quality chocolate ice cream
2 cups (500 ml) whole milk
¼ cup (40 g) dark chocolate chips
4 candied cherries

EQUIPMENT

Whisk or electric mixer
Blender
Pastry bag

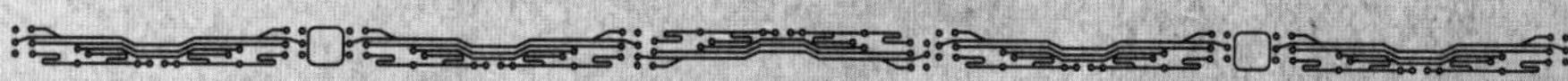

Start by preparing the whipped cream, which takes the most time. Chill a mixing bowl and mixer or electric whisk paddles in the freezer for 15 minutes beforehand. Chilling these elements ensures they are cold, aiding the cream's fat to crystallize for firmer whipped cream. Pour whipping cream and powdered sugar into the chilled mixing bowl. Whip vigorously until the cream thickens and rises. Set it aside in a cool place.

No sugar or syrup is added to our preparation, so opt for ice cream with high cocoa content. Blend chocolate ice cream and whole milk in a blender at maximum power for 2 minutes. Add dark chocolate chips and blend for an additional 1 minute (you won't reach 2.21 Gigawatts… apologies!).

For presentation, pour the chocolate mixture into 4 large milkshake glasses. Fill a piping bag with whipped cream and garnish each milkshake. Top each glass of whipped cream with a candied cherry. Now, your delightful old-fashioned milkshake is ready to be savored!

TS
MANAC
1950-2000
1950-2000
MANAC

STAR WARS

For **1 PINT GLASS** - Preparation: **5 MIN** - LEVEL ✦

Corellian ale is a classic in pubs all over the galaxy! Brewed directly on the planet Corellia, where General Solo was born, it's possible to prepare a powerful, spicy version: enough to stun a Wookiee or disconcert the brave Sabacc players you might be toasting with!

A CORELLIA
Whiskey, amber beer and cumin

INGREDIENTS

1 shot of RedBreast 12-year-old whiskey
Pale ale (amber beer)
1 pinch cumin

EQUIPMENT

Shot

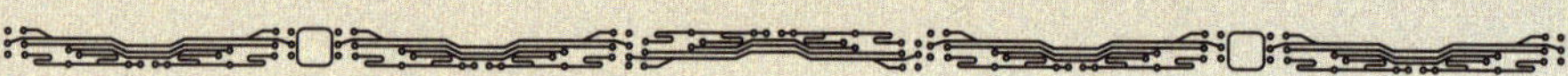

Pour the Redbreast whiskey into a shot glass.

Hold the shot glass in one hand and invert the empty pint glass over the top. Position the shot glass at the bottom of the pint and flip the entire setup upside down. This places the shot at the bottom of the pint glass.

Fill the pint glass to the brim with amber beer and sprinkle a pinch of cumin over the foam. While tilting the pint glass as you drink, the shot will gradually rise, releasing the Redbreast whiskey into the beer.

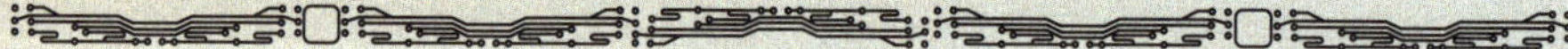

Serves 4 - Preparation: **20 MIN** - Cooking time: **1 H 10** - LEVEL ✦

DAGOBAH ROOT STEW
Vegetarian root vegetable stew

INGREDIENTS

5 carrots	1 shallot	3 juniper berries
4 turnips	4 cloves	⅔ tbsp (10 g) butter
2 parsnips	4 whole leeks	1 bouquet garni
½ celeriac	½ savoy cabbage	Salt and pepper
4 agria potatoes	1 tsp. coarse salt	
1 onion	8 cups (2 l) water	

Begin by preparing the vegetables. Peel the carrots, turnips, parsnips, celeriac, potatoes, onion, and shallot. Use cloves to stud the onion, then set it aside.

Trim any damaged leaves from the leeks and savoy cabbage. Rinse all the vegetables thoroughly.

Cut 4 carrots into large sticks, quarter the turnips, slice the parsnips into large pieces, cube the potatoes, halve the leeks, and divide the savoy cabbage into six sections.

Create an aromatic garnish by finely dicing the remaining carrot and shallot. You won't need a lightsaber for this; a regular knife will suffice.

In a saucepan, combine coarse salt and water, and bring it to a boil.

Meanwhile, heat a stewpot over medium heat. Toast the juniper berries until fragrant. Add butter, then the carrot and shallot brunoise. Sauté for 5 minutes without browning. Introduce all the other vegetables and the bouquet garni, immediately followed by the boiling salted water.

Simmer for 1 hour, stirring occasionally, until all the vegetables soften. Remove the pot from the heat once the vegetables meld.

Take out the clove-studded onion and bouquet garni. Set the vegetables aside and strain the broth to obtain a clear stock.

Presentation: Arrange pieces of each vegetable in 4 wooden bowls and cover them with the clear broth for serving.

DUNE

A coffee whose fragrant properties, lightly flavored with spice, will enable you to withstand the rigors of the Arrakis climate. Here's how it was prepared by some of my Fremen brothers, and how Muad'dib is said to have appreciated it.

ARRAKEEN COFFEE SPECIAL
Cinnamon cappuccino

INGREDIENTS

¾ cup (200 ml) milk
2 cinnamon sticks
2 ½ cups (600 ml) fresh water
4 tbsp ground Arabica coffee
Honey (optional)
1 tsp ground cinnamon

EQUIPMENT

Piston coffee maker
Strainer
Milk frother or emulsifier

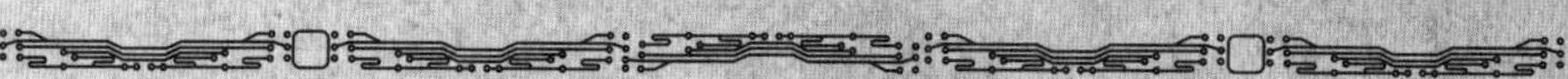

➤ Pour the milk into a saucepan and add the cinnamon sticks. Bring the milk to a gentle boil, then let the cinnamon infuse for a few minutes.

➤ Take the saucepan off the heat and prepare the coffee. Opt for a pure Ethiopian Arabica, known for its rich flavor profile with subtle hints of cocoa. Add 4 tablespoons of coffee to the coffee maker.

➤ Heat fresh water in a saucepan until it starts to simmer. Pour the hot water over the coffee grounds in the pot.

➤ Using a teaspoon, gently stir the coffee into the water. Keep the plunger in the raised position and allow the coffee to brew in the water for 1 minute 30 seconds to 2 minutes.

➤ While the coffee brews, strain the milk through a strainer and froth it using a milk frother or emulsifier. Set it aside and return to your coffee maker. Gradually lower the plunger, filtering out the coffee grounds without applying excessive force.

For serving: Pour the brewed coffee into individual cups. If desired, sweeten with honey to taste. Using a spoon, delicately layer the flavored milk foam on top of the coffee. Finish by sprinkling a touch of ground cinnamon. Enjoy!

For 1 **SQUARE TUMBLER** - Preparation: **5 MIN** - LEVEL ✦

SEXY BLUE BOX
Tequila, Parfait Amour and curaçao

INGREDIENTS

8 tsp (40 ml) tequila
1 tsp Parfait Amour cocktail liqueur
4 tsp (20 ml) curaçao
½ cup (150 ml) lemonade
Ice cubes

EQUIPMENT

Boston shaker

✈ Pour all the ingredients, excluding the lemonade, into a shaker glass. Stir vigorously for 30 seconds.

✈ Strain the contents of the shaker into a square tumbler glass. Finish by topping it off with lemonade. Your zany star cocktail is now ready to be enjoyed!

TERMINATOR

For 1 JULEP GLASS - Preparation: **10 MIN** - LEVEL ✦

SARAKONOR 0101001101000001010100100010000 010100101101001111010011001001111010010010

Gin, absinthe, brandy and cherry liqueur

INGREDIENTS

4 tsp (20 ml) gin
4 tsp (20 ml) absinthe
4 tsp (20 ml) brandy
4 tsp (20 ml) cherry liqueur
Crushed ice

EQUIPMENT

Cocktail spoon

Pour the gin, absinthe, and brandy into a julep glass.

Add crushed ice, then using a cocktail spoon, stir to blend the spirits.

Top it up once more with crushed ice and pour cherry liqueur over the top for a bloody effect. Now you're prepared to raise a toast to the Machines!

0100000101110101011011001101000010000001010010011011110110001001100101011100100111010001100010010000001110010011001010111011001101000010
1110110011000010110110001000001101111011001100010000001110100011010000110010010010000001001010110000101100011011010000110100101101110011
1001010000101001001101011010110110101011011001000001001010110100101101011000011011010000110100101101110011
0000001110000011100011000011101010010110110001010001000000110100010101000001001110100011010000100011011101001010010010010011
0000001000000110110101011010010101101100111010010111010001001010111001010010100110010110011001011011100110011011101100101100011101010010110011
0010110010100110101101011011011010001010010111011000001001010011010001010110001010011110110101011001001001010011100011010001
010010100001101001001010010110010110110000010000110100011010001110110110010011001100111011011011000111001010000011010001001
101101100001000000010010011100010010100001010100010110011010011010011001110110101010001100101010111010001001001010101001100110
0110011011011010001000000011000110010011011000100011000101000011010011011101100101001001001110001011101010110011011001101001100110
1100101011010011011001010101001010010110010001010011011010001101010011001001001001010101010101001101101010001000001001010110101101010100100
1001010010000011100000110101010101101100100110010010010001110100000010000000110011010010010010000010010110001010100101101010010100110010001
0010011110100010010001001010011000010101100011010101100001101101000011010010010110101001100101010100011010101110110101110100100110
0000011110100010101101010010010110000010000011011010101010100110001101010101101001001001001000110010101001001110010001001100011011001001001
1100111010001101000010010010010000000110010101110100000000011011000110010010010001100010011100100110010001010110111001100100001110010010011
1011100100010000000100100100101010100101001000110010011011011000110001000001010010110101000100000011001101010101011010010010011001010100100
0010000001100101011101000001000011101000000110000010000110110010011100010000001001100101000010110101011001001001000010001001
1100101010001001101001101010100100011110110111010101000010010111110001010010001101110110111111011110111
0010101101001010010000110001011011110111010100101010011010101010110101100110010011001100100110001101000110
0010011100010110111101110010101010111100010010101111011001010111011001010111011000100010110011001
1001001010010010001001010001010101110110100101001001001010101001100110011011010001000000110000010101001
0010000010110101110100010010000011101000010000010000010011000110010011011101001000101101110110001001010010
1100100010000010000110011011001010110100010010000011001010101010101000011000010100110010010100010011001
0001011011110011001110110110011000001001001000011100000110000110001100011101010010101010001100010100101010010010010
0010110110011001001101000010000010001011100001100001110001100001110101001001010100011000101001010100100100101010
0011100001111011010010101001011001100100110010010001110100000010000000110011010010010010000010010110001010100101
0100000101010101001010010110010110011001011011100110011011101100101100011101010010

Serves 4 - Preparation: **5 MIN** - LEVEL ✦

DATTA BYDOS
Date, mango and almond milk

INGREDIENTS

1 ⅔ cup (250 g) fresh dates
1 small mango
2 cups (500 ml) milk
6 ⅔ tbsp (100 ml) almond milk

EQUIPMENT

Blender

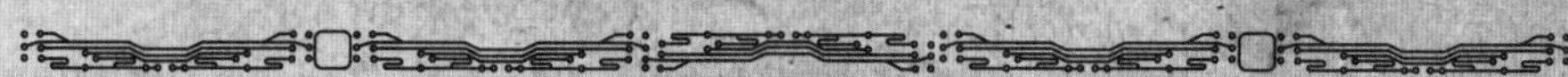

Prepare the fruit by halving the dates with a paring knife and removing the pits. Keep the dates aside.

Using a knife, peel the mango. Cut one half into substantial pieces, ensuring nothing is left on the pit to avoid waste.

Dice the other half into brunoise, creating 0.5 cm cubes, to be used for garnishing. Set the diced mango aside.

In a blender, combine the pitted dates, mango pieces, and milk. Blend vigorously for 2 minutes. Add the almond milk and blend for an additional minute to create a smooth emulsion.

For garnishing: Pour the freshly blended fruit juice into 4 glasses and arrange the diced mango on the surface. Enjoy your refreshing drink!

THANKS MORE
SEND

H2G2

PAN GALACTIC GARGLE BLASTER
Chartreuse, génépi, Get 27, mint, etc.

INGREDIENTS

Absinthe spray
4 tsp (20 ml) anisette
4 tsp (20 ml) Chartreuse
4 tsp (20 ml) génépi
3 ⅓ tbsp (50 ml) sparkling water
2 tsp (10 ml) Get 27
A few sprigs of mint
Crushed ice

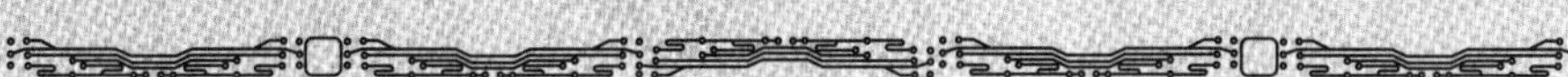

Spritz the inside of the tumbler glass with 2 sprays of absinthe. Swirl crushed ice in the glass to chill it.

Discard the ice and pour the anisette, Chartreuse, and génépi into the glass.

Top it up with sparkling water.

Carefully pour Get 27 over the mixture to create a green fallout effect.

Garnish the drink with mint, gently tapping it against the glass rim to release its aroma. Enjoy your concoction!

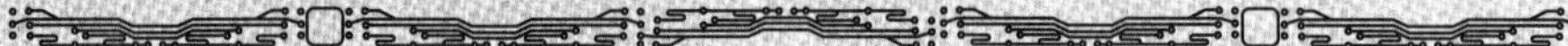

ALIEN

THE EIGHTH PASSENGER
Guinness, ginger and jasmine

INGREDIENTS

2 tsp (10 ml) ginger syrup
2 tsp (10 ml) jasmine syrup
2 cups (500 ml) Guinness
8 Xenomorph Acid beads (ginger syrup beads + lemon juice)

Referring to our tips on page 43, you'll discover how to create flavored marbles.

Prepare marbles using ginger syrup and lemon juice. The combination of these two creates an extremely acidic mix, hence we've named them Xenomorph Acid.

Pour ginger syrup and jasmine syrup into a pint glass. Then, in two separate batches, pour in the Guinness. Gently position the Acid marbles on top of the foam. Watch them slowly descend into the darkness of the liquid, and quietly savor the moment.

SCIENCE-FICTION
Lexicon

B

ALE BEER

Top-fermented, medium-alcohol beer.

BOUQUET GARNI

A collection of aromatic herbs tied into small bundles and used as seasoning. It is generally composed of thyme, bay leaf and a leek leaf.

BRUNOISE

Cutting vegetables into 0.5 cm cubes.

C

CHARTREUSE

Herbal liqueur produced in Voiron, Isère, by the monks of the Grande Chartreuse, whose composition is kept secret.

G

GUINNESS

A top-fermented dark beer of Irish origin, made from heavily roasted malt.

R

REDBREAST WHISKEY

58% Irish whiskey, powerful and spicy on the palate.

ROASTING

Frying a food (usually dry), such as coffee beans, almonds or cloves, without fat, to release its aromas.

RYE WHISKEY

American whiskey whose main ingredient is rye.

HYDRATING DATES

Dates come in numerous varieties, with the Deglet Nour date from Algeria, originally from North Africa or India, known for its exceptional taste.

To facilitate blending, especially with dried dates, rehydration is essential. One method involves steaming the dates for 5 minutes to revive their soft and fleshy texture.

Alternatively, you can soak the dried dates in water for 3 hours prior to use so that they regain moisture and pliability.

WHIPPED CREAM WITH SIPHON

Sometimes it's easier to use a siphon to make mousse, cream or espuma. Here's how to make Chantilly cream with a siphon.

INGREDIENTS
FOR A 0.5 L SIPHON CAPACITY
1 ½ cup (400 ml) cream, minimum 35% fat content
2 tbsp (15 g) powdered sugar

Begin by unscrewing the siphon and ensuring the bowl is clean before moving on to prepare the cream.

Combine the cream and powdered sugar in a mixing bowl. Whisk thoroughly to blend. For a smoother texture, strain the mixture through a fine chinois strainer. This step is crucial to prevent any potential clogging of the siphon by impurities such as starch in the sugar.

Once strained, pour the mixture into the siphon tank and securely screw it back on. Insert a nitrous oxide cartridge (the silver N2O cartridges) into the cannula and tighten it until you hear the distinct sound of gas releasing into the tank.

Please note, attempting to unscrew the siphon afterward may result in a cream explosion.

Vigorously shake the siphon to prepare your Chantilly cream. When dispensing onto your creations, invert the siphon and gently press the plunger to avoid forceful splashes.

Important information:

- Store the cream in the siphon in a cool place for up to 48 hours. Remember to clean the nozzle before refrigerating the siphon.

- Do not fill a 500 ml siphon with more than 400 ml of liquid.

- Typically, use 1 capsule for 500 ml of liquid or 2 capsules for 1 liter.

AGAR-AGAR BEADS, THE SPHERIFICATION OF A LIQUID

INGREDIENTS
6 ⅔ tbsp (100 ml) water
10 tbsp (150 ml) mint syrup
2 tsp (5 g) agar-agar
6 ⅔ (100 ml) rapeseed oil, previously refrigerated

- Begin by pouring water into a small saucepan. Add the mint syrup and thoroughly mix. Incorporate the agar-agar powder using a hand blender or whisk to ensure a well-blended mixture.

- Bring the combined ingredients to a brief boil, then remove the pan from heat. Once again, blend the mixture with a whisk or hand blender, allowing it to cool down to room temperature.

- Use a syringe or pipette to collect the liquid. Pour the cooled rapeseed oil into a glass, then slowly drip the liquid from the syringe or pipette into the oil-filled glass. This sudden temperature difference will cause the drops to gel, forming beads that will descend to the bottom of the glass.

- Using a spoon or skimmer, carefully remove the beads from the oil. Gently rinse them with clean water before incorporating them into your beverages.

Tip: For fruit or vegetable juice spheres, simply add 2% agar-agar to the liquid volume.

Dear reader,

Welcome to this collection of notes that I, the timeless Traveller of Worlds, have recorded during my fantastic explorations.
Before you read any further, I must warn you about two things:
- I love digressing.
- I love making lists (and brackets, so that's three things, reflecting my affinity with mathematics).

With that established, I'd like to start by telling you how my journey began.

One day, as I sat quietly on the terrace of a café, an eccentric (though notably courteous), individual put his hand on my shoulder and asked me if I had the soul of a traveller. I'd like to ask you the same question, my dear reader: do you feel up to the task of travelling the worlds, even the most unlikely? If the answer is no, and yet you're still standing here reading these lines, I must express my astonishment. If the answer is yes, then it's imperative that I reveal my "peremptory, albeit not entirely exhaustive, list of the most comfortable means of transport for world travellers".

Far be it from me to tell you all about it, as I know you'd be willing to untie your purse to buy one, but I will mention a few of the vehicles featured.

You'll be amazed to learn that the esteemed Doctor's fabulous T.A.R.D.I.S. comes a very distant third. A T.A.R.D.I.S. – standing for Time And Relative Dimension In Space – is a vessel designed and used by the Time Lord to travel through time and space.

A fantastic invention and would be perfect in every way, if it didn't have the unfortunate disadvantage of never being fully functional, of being difficult to maneuver on its own, and if it (or "she", for that matter) wasn't endowed with a personality that you won't be surprised to learn I didn't much like. On the other hand, the British series from which this ship originated, Doctor Who – broadcast on the BBC since 1963 – is fascinating and, although it has strayed from its original educational purpose, remains highly entertaining and magnificently imaginative.

I much prefer the quiet purring of large carriers such as the *USS Enterprise*, in which the *Star Trek* crew travels (an entire universe of series, films, novels, etc.), or that good big *USS Daedalus*, seen in the *Stargate Atlantis* series. The latter's size and charter often allow it to criss-cross space with serenity, which would have served Daniel Jackson and Jack O'Neil well when I came across them on that sandy planet, in the film that inaugurated the saga. Indeed, it's not uncommon to come across, at the turn of a galaxy, an uncharted extraterrestrial species whose evolution seemed to have no other purpose than to produce the most violent and unreasonable scum in the universe. The crew of the *USS Enterprise* NCC 1701, led by Captain Kirk, could tell you countless stories of their often hostile encounters with more or less intelligent alien life forms. And I'm not going to comment here on the SG-1 team's never-ending struggle against those pesky Goa'ulds.

For more modest wallets, a *Firefly*-class vessel should do the trick. Note that it has the unfortunate tendency to attract the attention of the Alliance, pirates and, to put it bluntly, all that the far reaches of the universe can produce as a source of boredom for a moderately respectable captain. Proof of this can be found in the adventures of Captain Malcolm Reynolds, aboard the *Serenity*, in Joss Whedon's *Firefly* series.

For greater peace and quiet and a dimension commensurate with your solitary journey, I prefer an X-Wing fighter (from *Star Wars*, which needs no introduction), perhaps even accompanied by an R2 astromech droid (though don't count on the conversation). Now that's a means of transport whose panache borders on insolence!

Mind you, in my many travels, no vehicle has impressed me with its cachet quite like the DeLorean (flying version) of the inventive Dr. Emmett Brown. As he himself says, it's got style! So much so, in fact, that it underwent several transformations over the course of the three installments of Robert Zemeckis' *Back to the Future* films. In fact, I rather like the retro look of the whitewall tires, don't you? A word about a vehicle that's probably a lot less practical, but awfully classy: the Terminator's Harley (in the second installment, *Terminator 2*, released in 1991). Admittedly, it won't get you as far as any of the other vehicles on this list, but it will do so with a bang. Besides, what's the point of traveling light-years if you can be the ultimate bad boy without leaving your neighborhood?

Come to think of it, and it would be dishonest of me not to mention it, while making it clear that it is with the deepest respect for my friend Paul Muad'dib and for the Fremen people that I write these words, I can't advise you to travel on the back of sand worms. If you find desert and sandy planets uncomfortable, you can be sure that crossing them on the back of a Shai-Hulud is even more so. Sure, the sensation of power and speed is exhilarating, but steering them is no mean feat! What possessed Frank Herbert to imagine such creatures in *Dune*? We wonder...

Finally, for a truly unprecedented, unpredictable and frankly incongruous experience, I recommend a trip aboard the Heart-in-Gold, which you'll find in Douglas Adams' book series, *The Hitchhiker's Guide to the Galaxy*. This incredible vessel is powered by an infinite improbability generator. This allows it to reach infinite speed, and will incidentally land you in highly improbable situations. Not impossible, just very very very improbable.

Ah, one final word of advice: whatever means of transport you choose, dear reader, be sure to check dark corners, ventilation ducts and any sneaky nooks and crannies that might harbor a discreet, lethal creature. Watch Ridley Scott's *Alien, the Eighth Passenger* to get an idea of the disastrous consequences should you omit this step.

Excuse me, reader? My story? Ah yes, how it all began! I'll get to that soon!

Fantasy

    For **1 GLASS** · Preparation: **5 MIN** · LEVEL ✦

VIVACITY POTION
OR HEALING POTION FOR INGROWN TOENAILS, I'M NOT SURE…

INGREDIENTS

2 tsp (10 ml) gin
2 tsp (10 ml) vodka
2 tsp (10 ml) white rum
2 tsp (10 ml) tequila
2 tsp (10 ml) triple sec
10 tbsp (150 ml) bissap juice (p. 69)
2 tbsp crushed ice

EQUIPMENT

Boston shaker

✜ Put the crushed ice in a Boston shaker, then pour in the gin, vodka, rum, tequila, and triple sec.

✜ Shake briskly, then pour it into the carpenter's bowl resting on the workbench at the back of the laboratory… or into an anchovy jar.

✜ Add the bissap juice atop the mixture, brought back by Sire Dagonet from his travels beyond the great southern desert. Mix thoroughly. Now you're ready to go.

For **1 TUMBLER GLASS** · Preparation: **5 MIN** · **LEVEL** ✦

Gadzooks! It's just that the cook's been around too much, and now this morning he's not quite up to the task of preparing the captain's gruel. CAN YOU HEAR ME, YOU BILGE RATS? One of you get to work and make me a tafia worthy of this ship and its captain!

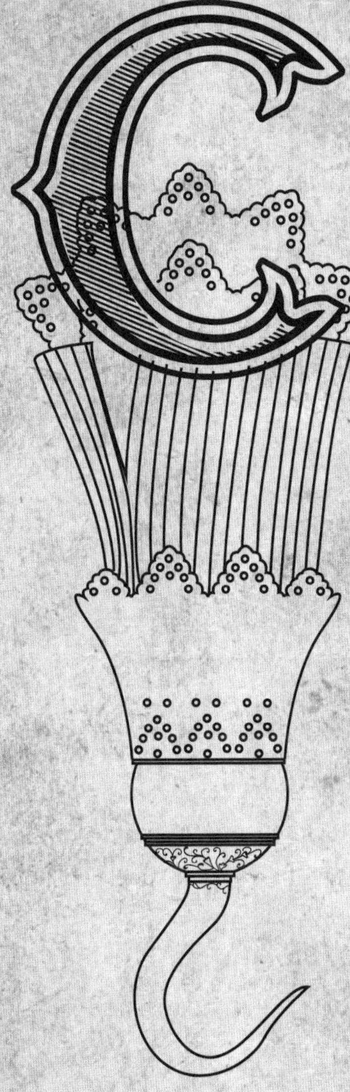

CROCODILE ISLAND
GOLD STRIKE, LIME AND MINT

INGREDIENTS

8 tsp (40 ml) Gold Strike
Juice of ½ lime
1 tsp cocktail agave syrup
8 to 10 mint leaves
10 tbsp (150 ml) tonic

EQUIPMENT

Shaker

✛ In a shaker, pour the Gold Strike and add the lime juice, then the agave syrup and 4 mint leaves.

✛ Shake briskly, then pour into a tumbler glass. Top up with tonic.

✛ Use the remaining mint leaves to garnish and flavor the drink.

For 4 GLASSES - Preparation: 1 H - LEVEL ✦

Here's a beverage with exotic flavors: a humble tribute to the dangerous journeys of a barbarian in search of glory and the blood of his enemies.

CIMMERIAN WARRIOR TEA
INFUSION OF HIBISCUS, GINGER AND RED BERRIES

INGREDIENTS

4 cups (1 l) water
20 dried hibiscus flowers
⅔ tbsp (10 g) chopped ginger
½ cup (100 g) blackberries
½ cup (100 g) strawberries
½ cup (100 g) sugar

EQUIPMENT

Chinois strainer

✜ Pour the water into a saucepan and add the hibiscus, ginger, and berries. Bring it to a boil and then remove it from the heat.

✜ Allow the infusion to cool down.

✜ Strain the mixture through a sieve, pressing the fruit to extract as much juice as possible. Add the sugar and mix thoroughly. Keep it aside in a cool place.

Serving suggestions: Fill four 25 cl glasses to the brim, as Conan's thirst is not easily quenched. He'll be surprised by the sweetness of the fruit and the warmth of the ginger combined with tangy hibiscus!

Conan is a character from a novel created in 1932 by Robert E. Howard, which was later adapted for the big screen, notably in 1982 by John Milius (starring Arnold Schwarzenegger). It narrates the adventurous tale of Conan, an accomplished Cimmerian warrior, muscular and agile. However, it would be reductive to label him merely a mindless "barbarian", as he is a skilled tactician, cunning, and fluent in several languages. Nonetheless, it's understandable if one imagines him wielding a sword and vanquishing his foes with force.

For 4 TULIP GLASSES OF DAIKINI · Preparation: 10 MIN · Rest: 6 H · LEVEL ✦

No brave man would leave Ufgood Reach to set out on an adventure without proper equipment. Nor would any brave man leave without a little pick-me-up. Here's the recipe for a spiced wine that the Great Aldwin himself is said to have loved! Just make sure you don't inadvertently slip any magic acorns into it, as the texture of your spiced wine could end up... rocky!

M EEGOSH'S TONIC
SPICED WINE

INGREDIENTS

4 cups (1 l) red wine
⅓ cup (100 g) honey
3 cinnamon sticks
5 cardamom pods
5 cloves
2 tsp ground ginger

EQUIPMENT

Sieve

✤ Pour the red wine and honey into a saucepan. Stir with a spatula until the honey blends perfectly with the wine. Then add the cinnamon, cardamom, cloves and ground ginger.

✤ Bring to the boil, then remove from the heat.

✤ Cover and leave to infuse for at least 6 hours.

✤ Strain to a clear liquid and fill a small carafe or 4 tulip-shaped glasses. You can drink the spiced wine at room temperature, or warm it for a few moments over a campfire before enjoying! And don't forget to bring plenty of water in case you come across a Daikini locked in a cage...

Willow is a 1988 film by Ron Howard, based on an idea by George Lucas. It recounts the adventures of Willow, a small Nelwyn who crosses paths with baby Elora. This little human girl has a destiny that Willow will help her fulfill, in a world of magic, fairies and fierce warriors. This work has become a classic: who doesn't remember the wicked Bavmorda, the magician Fin Raziel's metamorphosis or those magic acorns?

For 4 MINI TUREENS · Preparation: 25 MIN · Cooking: 40 MIN · LEVEL ✦ ✦

DANVERT CREAM

CREAM OF ASPARAGUS IN A CRUST

INGREDIENTS

3 bunches fresh asparagus
4 spring onions
4 tbsp olive oil
4 cups (1 l) ready-to-use
poultry stock cube or powder
⅔ cup (150 ml) whipping
cream

1 ¾ tbsp (25 g) butter
½ pound (200 g) ready-to-use
or homemade puff pastry
(p. 68)
1 egg yolk
Salt and freshly ground
pepper

EQUIPMENT

Hand blender
Kitchen brush

✠ The day before, prepare the puff pastry (p. 68) if you have chosen to make it yourself.

✠ Using a vegetable peeler, peel the asparagus. Cut into pieces and set aside. Peel and finely chop the spring onions. Set aside. Clean your work surface, and don't leave any peelings lying around. You know how much Danvert likes La Renardière to be well-kept, especially his kitchens!

✠ Heat the olive oil in a casserole dish, then add the asparagus and onion pieces and sauté over medium heat for 3 to 4 minutes (be careful not to brown the onions!).

✠ Season with salt and pepper and stir in the chicken stock. Bring to the boil and simmer for 20 minutes. Set aside off the heat.

✠ Blend the cream for 1 minute, until it thickens, then stir it lightly into the pan and add the butter.

✠ Using a hand blender, blend the contents of the saucepan. Check and adjust the seasoning if necessary: you don't want to meet Messire Ballardieu's eyes if the soup he's served isn't properly seasoned…

✠ Preheat the oven to 210°C (gas mark 7).

✠ Now take the homemade or ready-to-use puff pastry out of the fridge. Shape into 4 small balls and roll out separately to make 4 discs. Pour the asparagus cream into 4 mini-soup tureens and cover each tureen with puff pastry. Brush with egg yolk and place in the oven for 15 minutes. Remove from oven and enjoy.

 For **4 PINTS** · Preparation: **30 MIN** · Cooking: **5 to 10 MIN** · LEVEL ✦ ✦ ✦

BUTTERBEER RESTYLED
LAGER, CIDER, BUTTER, VANILLA AND CINNAMON

INGREDIENTS

½ cup (100 g) butter
4 cups (1 l) vanilla ice cream
3 ½ tsp (10 g) ground cinnamon
1 ⅓ tbsp (20 ml) cane sugar syrup
1 cup (250 ml) sweet apple cider
3 cups (750 ml) lager
1 ⅔ cup (400 ml) caramelized whipped cream (p. 69)

❈ Melt the butter in a saucepan over very low heat. Once the butter has almost melted, add the ice cream (still over very low heat). Stir gently until the cream is fully incorporated and the mixture is smooth.

❈ Add the cinnamon and cane sugar syrup. Continue stirring, then add the cider and beer.

❈ Bring the mixture to a gentle boil for 2 minutes, then remove the pan from the heat.

To serve: pour hot or cold butterbeer into pints. Top each beer with caramel whipped cream and enjoy!

ADVAN

HARRY POTTER

For **1 CHAMPAGNE FLUTE** - Preparation: **10 MIN** - LEVEL ✦ *FOR A POTION WITH A LIMITED EFFECTIVENESS OF 3 MIN*

Far from being comparable to sorcerer Zygmunt Budge's original version, which took six long months to prepare, this Liquid Luck solution can be prepared in just a few minutes: on the other hand, it will give you only 3 minutes of extraordinary luck, at most.

LIQUID LUCK
POTION OF GIN, ORANGE LIQUEUR AND CHAMPAGNE

INGREDIENTS

8 tsp (40 ml) Beefeater gin
4 tsp (20 ml) orange liqueur
2 tsp (10 ml) cane sugar syrup
3 ⅓ tbsp (50 ml) champagne
Crushed ice

EQUIPMENT

Boston shaker

✤ Pour the gin, orange liqueur and cane sugar syrup into a Boston shaker. Add crushed ice and shake vigorously.

✤ Pour the contents of the shaker into a champagne flute or medium-sized bottle, filtering out the crushed ice.

✤ Top up with champagne. Not so difficult to prepare, is it? Don't tell Professor Slughorn, he might get offended!

For 1 PINT - Preparation: 5 MIN - LEVEL ✦

You're just moments away from a good fight between friends... But why not refresh yourself with a drink worthy of the Feegle that you are?

Nac Mac Micmac

CARDHU, WHISKEY CREAM AND AMBER BEER

INGREDIENTS

8 tsp (40 ml) Cardhu (or another scented Scotch whisky)
4 tsp (20 ml) whiskey cream
1 ½ cup (400 ml) Scottish amber ale

❄ Pour the Scotch whiskey and cream of whiskey into a pint. Top up with beer to the brim.

Enjoy this great beverage, it may well be the last time you drink it... YAAAAAAAAAH!

THE LORD OF THE RINGS

ENT DRAUGHT

WOODY INFUSION, ROOIBOS AND MARE GIN

INGREDIENTS

6 ⅔ tbsp (100 ml) cold mineral water
1 pinch rooibos tea leaves
8 tsp (40 ml) Mare gin
4 tsp (20 ml) elderflower liqueur
1 sprig rosemary
Crushed ice

EQUIPMENTS

Tea ball
Mixing glass
Julep filter

✠ Place your bowl in the fridge to chill before serving. Heat the water in a saucepan.

✠ Put a pinch of rooibos tea leaves in a tea ball and place it in a cup. Pour the simmering water over the tea and let it infuse for 3 minutes. Remove the tea ball and let it cool for 20 minutes at room temperature.

✠ Pour the gin into a mixing glass. Add the liqueur and 40 ml of cooled rooibos tea.

✠ Add crushed ice to fill half of the mixing glass and stir. Then, add more ice and stir again.

✠ Take your cooled bowl and pour the contents of the mixing glass into it, filtering the mixture with a julep filter.

✠ Garnish the bowl with a sprig of rosemary, one of the essential herbs of Mare gin, perfectly complementing the gin and the woody tones of the tea.

A literary reference in contemporary fantasy, The Lord of the Rings *is a three-volume saga following J.R.R. Tolkien's* The Hobbit. *With this woody, invigorating blend, we aimed to emphasize the ecological message conveyed by the work: mentioning the Ents and the Sylvan lands traversed by the heroes of Tolkien's novels felt important.*

After a night of drinking in the company of your friend Ulfgar, you wake up with quite a headache: your dwarf friends are still sound asleep, as you can tell by the chorus of snoring around you. You move to retrieve your gear: a sealed parchment protrudes slightly from your bag. You pick it up. Here's what it says:

"A promise made, a promise kept. Here is recorded the secret of the sacred brew that my ancestors have passed down for hundreds of years. Here is the secret for which many adventurers would kill. Know, young traveller, that if this secret ever gets out, I'll find you, strangle you with my bare hands and dig into your insides with my axe. Then I'll feast on your still-smoldering carcass.

Best regards,

Ulfgar"

DWARF BEER FROM THE FORGOTTEN REALMS
WARM BEER WITH SPICES

INGREDIENTS

8 egg yolks
½ cup (100 g) brown sugar
3 cloves
2 star anises
3 ½ tsp (10 g) ground ginger
8 cups (2 l) lager
Juice from 1 orange

EQUIPMENT

Chinois strainer

✠ In a saucepan off the heat, pour the egg yolks, then add the sugar and whisk until the mixture whitens.

✠ Continuing to whisk, incorporate the cloves, star anise, and ground ginger until smooth. Then, pour in the beer and orange juice.

✠ Simmer over low heat, ensuring the beer never reaches boiling point. Once hot, strain the mixture through a strainer and pour into 4 pints.

FANTASY *Tips*

PUFF PASTRY

INGREDIENTS FOR 2 ⅕ CUPS (500 G) OF DOUGH
6 ⅔ tbsp (100 ml) fresh water
⅓ tsp (2 g) fine salt
1 ½ cup (200 g) flour
1 ⅕ cup (250 g) butter at room temperature

My friends, here's a preparation that will require technique and patience, but which, with the right training, you will perfect in no time!

• Prepare a basic batter by combining salt water and flour. Start by pouring 50 ml of fresh water into a glass and add the salt. In a bowl, pour the flour, followed by the fresh salted water, and the remaining fresh water. Use your hands to gently incorporate the water into the flour, avoiding excessive kneading.

• Shape the mixture into a ball and slightly flatten it. Wrap it in cling film and refrigerate it for 2 hours. Once chilled, set it aside at room temperature for a few moments while you prepare the butter for kneading.

• Soften the butter by hand or with a spatula until it reaches the same consistency as the mixture. Set it aside. Sprinkle a bit of flour onto the work surface to prevent the dough from sticking. Place the ball of dough on the floured surface and, using a knife, create a cross on the dough, then pull the edges apart.

• With a rolling pin, extend each end of the dough to about 2 cm thick, leaving a raised section in the center. Pour the softened butter over this raised portion and fold over each end to encase the butter.

• Roll out the dough gently to maintain the butter within it, extending it to three times its original length while maintaining its width. Fold the dough into thirds and turn it 90°—this marks the first "turn" for your dough. It's these turns that create the layers in puff pastry.

• Repeat this process. After the second turn, let the dough rest in cling film in the fridge for 2 hours. Remove it and complete 2 more turns. Continue until you have completed a total of 6 turns for the perfect puff pastry, then let it rest in the fridge for an additional hour. You've just made homemade puff pastry!

SALTED BUTTER CARAMEL COULIS

INGREDIENTS
FOR 1 CUP (250 ML)
OF COULIS
4 ½ tbsp (65 g) semi-salted butter
¾ cup (200 ml) liquid cream
⅔ cup (120 g) sugar

• Begin by cutting the semi-salted butter into small cubes and set them aside.

• Take a saucepan and warm the liquid cream over medium heat.

• Simultaneously, prepare a dry caramel (without water): in another saucepan, melt the sugar until it reaches a beautiful amber color. Turn off the heat and carefully pour in the lukewarm cream.

• Gently reheat the mixture over low heat and introduce the cubes of semi-salted butter. Whisk the ingredients together until they become smooth and homogeneous.

FANTASY Lexicon

C

CARAMEL WHIPPED CREAM

To add flavor to your whipped cream, simply mix the cream with syrup, fruit coulis, flavoring or even caramel. This is how we like to make the caramel whipped cream we use as a topping on our homemade Butterbeer.

INGREDIENTS
1 ⅕ cup (300 ml) cream, minimum 35% fat content
6 ⅔ tbsp (100 ml) caramel coulis

Follow the whipped cream recipe (p. 43), replacing the powdered sugar with the caramel coulis.

Remember to filter the preparation well before placing it in the vat.

G

GIN

Grain brandy of Anglo-Saxon origin.

GOLD STRIKE

A cinnamon-based liqueur, recognizable by the gold flakes it contains.

M

MIXING GLASS

A glass used to spoon drinks or preparations that should not be shaken. It allows you to blend ingredients "smoothly", without diluting them too much in ice cubes.

P

PRESENTATION

Arranging a preparation on a serving dish or plate with taste and aesthetic appeal.

S

SET ASIDE

Putting aside a food preparation or an ingredient during cooking so that it can be used later.

T

TEQUILA

Mexican brandy produced by fermenting and distilling agave fruit.

BISSAP JUICE

Here's the kind of thing Conan might have discovered on his many travels: a juice scented with hibiscus flower and mint.

INGREDIENTS FOR 1 L OF BISSAP JUICE
3 ⅓ cups (150 g) dried hibiscus flowers
2 packets vanilla sugar
4 cups (1 l) water
1 dozen fresh mint leaves

• Rinse the hibiscus flowers and drain.

• Put them in a saucepan, then add the vanilla sugar. Pour in the water, stir and bring to the boil for 20 minutes. Remove the pan from the heat and add the mint. Leave to infuse until the mixture has cooled.

• Filter and bottle the juice. Place the bottles in the fridge for fresh consumption.

So, reader, where was I?

Ah, yes! That man who stopped me while I was drinking a strong coffee and asked me if I had the soul of a traveller! Well, my dear reader, if you don't know me yet, you should know that nothing makes me happier than the discovery of new things, be they geographical, scientific or of some other nature, definable or not.
We spent a few hours talking, and it soon became clear to me that this man was going to change my life. He must have seen in me the adventurer I was and offered me the chance to travel with him. What I didn't know was that this journey would be wonderful.

Speaking of travel, you, my reader, must be aware of the importance of rest, especially on endless journeys through exotic lands. I could go on at length about the shady encounters on planets at the edge of the universe, but I think it would be more useful for you to know my good addresses for eating after rescuing a princess (which is the sufficient and necessary condition to legitimately bear the title of "adventurer"*) or defeating a dragon.
So, without further ado, here's my "invaluable list of the most frequented taverns, provided your vaccinations are up to date".

First and foremost, I'd like to tell you what makes a tavern worthy of the name:

1. Good beer. Please note that "good" does not refer to taste, which is far too subjective for any sensible beer steward to take into account. My definition of a good beer is as follows: "Probably non-toxic liquid, varying in color from dirty brown to golden piss, whose alcohol content is indexed to the cleanliness of the establishment and whose cost justifies its place at the very top of the menu."

2. A tavern-keeper endlessly wiping dishes of relative hygiene (not least because his cloth harbors a bacteriological concentration lethal to 99% of known species).

3. An architecture that makes it impossible to fully illuminate this small, isolated table at which a hooded figure is invariably seated.

4. A clientele sufficiently civilized and refined to make a chaotic brawl unlikely. You'll have noticed that the presence of girly, corseted waitresses is not one of the criteria, at the express request of a reader from the Aries mountains.

* It should be noted, however, that there are no real prerequisites for the title of "princess", as many adventurers have learned to their cost.

Speaking of which, and since I'm talking about the Aries Mountains, the famous region featured in the late Terry Pratchett's *Discworld* universe, if you want to get a good first idea of a typical multiverse tavern, head for the *Tambour Rafistolé*, in Ankh-Morpork. Be warned, however, that this may well be the last idea you ever have. The establishment has notoriously had to undergo several repairs, and the attitude of some restless customers is no stranger to this.

For a quieter, though no less dangerous tasting experience, *La Tête de Sanglier* in Hogsmeade is a good place to go, provided you can get in (it's understood that all Hogwarts students—(including the famous Harry Potter)—are allowed to go there—but that doesn't mean they MUST). Bring your own glasses. Just because you have the opportunity to visit J.K. Rowling's work doesn't make you any less of a Muggle, so be warned!

In the unlikely event that your parental instincts haven't prevented you from travelling with your children, we can only recommend a trip to Neverland (the fabulous world of Peter Pan, revisited in Steven Spielberg's film *Hook*), where the songs of pirates will lead you to a little-known tavern that, let's face it, deserves to stay that way. But you won't be risking your life as much as you would elsewhere. How to get there: second star to the right and straight on until morning.

If you're looking for a starting point for an epic adventure, simply visit a tavern from the *Dungeons & Dragons* role-playing universe. Any tavern. Literally. It must be one of the immutable laws of physics in this world that taverns, no matter how modest or remote, are bound to welcome a mysterious contact in search of a group of adventurers who are obviously incompetent, don't get along and are clearly united solely by the lure of gain.

Finally, if prestige is your goal, then the noblest establishment I can recommend is the tavern in the village near Kaamelott castle, which, it's true, is so lacking in its usual clientele that it's easy to gain prestige. Not surprisingly, you'll come across several knights of the Round Table as imagined by Alexandre Astier.

I don't know if it belongs here, but I can't make this list without telling you about this little inn, whose name I couldn't remember, lost in the heart of the faubourg Saint-Antoine: there was nothing special about this place, except that its backyard was where Almadès, a Spanish fencing master, gave his fencing lessons. Rumor had it that this backyard was as good as any in the capital. In Paris of the year 1633 depicted in Pierre Pevel's work, I had the honor of meeting his closest companions: Baillardieu the feaster, Marciac the flirt, Baroness Agnès de Vaudreuil, sublime and fatal. All members of the Lames du Cardinal, an elite unit led by Captain Étienne de La Fargue on behalf of Cardinal de Richelieu. It was at their headquarters, La Renardière, that I had the pleasure of spending some wild evenings, between gastronomy and French wine, swords and dragonnets.

MANGA

For **4 CUPS** - Preparation: **10 MIN** - LEVEL ✦

Humanity is on the brink of extinction. There's no way of knowing when the Titans will assault the Wall again, and the next expedition outside the walls announced for my battalion won't take place for at least two days… It'll be the 57th, I think. Why not take the time to prepare a fragrant, powerful and… invigorating tea, as the Master Corporal likes it?

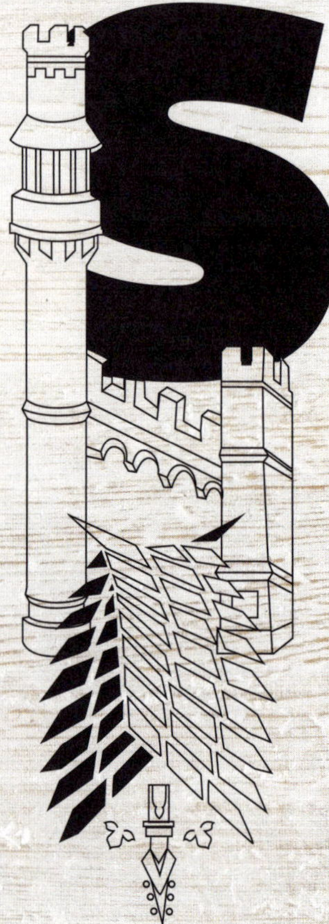

SOUVENIR OF SHIGANSHINA
EARL GREY, PLUM WINE AND BLACKCURRANT LIQUEUR

INGREDIENTS

3 ⅓ cups (800 ml) mineral water
6 ⅓ tsp (15 g) Earl Grey tea
⅔ cup (160 ml) plum wine
⅓ cup (80 ml) blackcurrant liqueur
Honey (optional)

EQUIPMENT

Pastry thermometer

🌸 Begin by preparing the Earl Grey tea: heat the water to 75°C (using a baking thermometer). Place the tea in its filter and immerse it in the water, allowing it to infuse for 2 to 3 minutes. Once infused, remove the filter from the water and set the tea aside for a brief period.

🌸 Proceed to pour 40 ml of plum wine into each cup, followed by 20 ml of blackcurrant liqueur.

🌸 Next, pour in 200 ml of hot tea and thoroughly stir the concoction. Take your time to relish this beverage and consider sweetening it with honey according to your taste.

Perhaps not as canonical as some of the works we've already covered in Gastronogeek, Attack on Titan (Shingeki no Kyojin) is a shōnen manga written and drawn by Hajime Isayama, published in Japan by Kodansha. This highly acclaimed manga unfolds in a world where humanity is no longer the dominant species. Massive and relentless Titans roam the Earth, devouring any humans they encounter. To survive, humans construct colossal walls around their cities. The story follows Eren Yaeger, a young fighter with remarkable powers, as he battles to reclaim human territory, seek revenge for his family, and unravel the mysteries surrounding the Titans.

   For 4 SMOOTHIE GLASSES · Preparation: **10 MIN** · Cooking: **30 MIN** · LEVEL ✦ ✦

It's hard to match the power and energy generated by Son Goku! Here's a smoothie that's worth every senzu you can find: tone, energy and power, all concentrated in one glass.

KAMEHAKAROT
CARROT, ORANGE AND GINGER SMOOTHIE

INGREDIENTS

1 pound (500 g) carrots
6 cups (1.5 l) sparkling water
Juice from 6 oranges
⅔ tbsp (10 g) chopped ginger
2 tbsp honey
3 or 4 ice cubes

EQUIPMENT

Blender

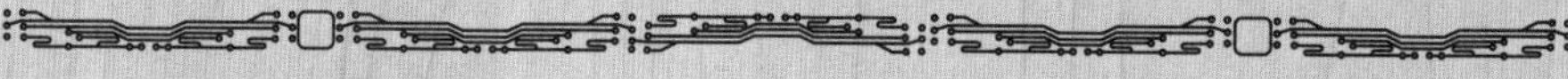

✿ Prepare the carrots by rinsing, peeling, and cutting them into large chunks.

✿ In a saucepan, bring the sparkling water to a boil and place the carrots in it.

✿ Let them cook for 30 minutes until they completely soften. Once done, drain them and set aside.

✿ Into a blender, pour the orange juice, chopped ginger, honey, carrots, and ice cubes. Blend the mixture for 1 minute and 30 seconds to 2 minutes to achieve a smooth emulsion, ensuring all the ingredients are thoroughly blended.

✿ Here's a refreshing drink that'll give you the strength to conquer mountains... or perhaps scale that towering structure over yonder with just your hands...

Serves 4 - Preparation: **20 MIN** - Cooking: **20 MIN** - LEVEL ✦ ✦ ✦

RAMEN ICHIRAKU

TONKOTSU RAMEN, WITH SPINACH, EGGS AND NARUTOMAKI

INGREDIENTS

¼ cup (40 g) narutomaki
5 ¼ cups (100 g) fresh spinach leaves
4 cups (1 l) sparkling water
4 eggs

4 pork cutlets, ⅓ pound (150 g) each
1 cup (250 ml) soy sauce
½ cup (150 ml) oyster sauce
2 ½ tsp (5 g) chopped ginger
1 clove garlic, minced
4 spring onions

½ cup (100 g) bamboo shoots
1 tsp olive oil
¾ pound (400 g) udon noodles
8 cups (2 l) tonkotsu broth (pork bone broth) (p. 97)
4 nori leaves

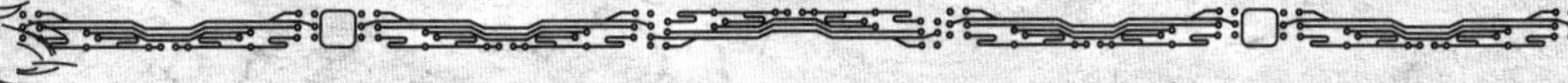

Prepare the garnishes for the ramen. Slice the narutomaki into thin strips and set them aside. Rinse the spinach thoroughly and drain it well. Bring the sparkling water to a boil and immerse the spinach for 5 minutes. Drain it thoroughly, fold it over, and then squeeze out any excess water using your hands. Use a paring knife to cut the spinach into 4 cm lengths and set it aside.

For the eggs, place them in a pot of boiling water for 4 minutes, then transfer them immediately into a bowl of iced water to halt the cooking process. Peel, slice them in half, and set them aside.

Now, prepare the pork cutlets by combining soy sauce, oyster sauce, chopped ginger, and garlic in a saucepan. Add the pork cutlets and cook over medium-high heat until they are fully cooked. Once done, remove the pork from the pan, let it rest briefly, and then slice it thinly. Set it aside.

Rinse the spring onions and bamboo shoots. Slice the onions in half lengthwise and cut the bamboo shoots into strips. Brush a frying pan with olive oil and quickly fry the vegetables for a few minutes to retain their crispness. Set aside the vegetables and proceed to cook the noodles.

In a large saucepan, bring 2 liters of salted water to a boil. Once boiling, add the udon noodles. As soon as it returns to a boil, pour a glass of cold water into the pan. When it begins to boil again, remove the pan from the heat and drain the noodles.

Finally, gently bring the tonkotsu broth to a boil. Arrange the noodles into 4 large bowls and cover them with the pork bone broth. Arrange the spring onions, bamboo shoots, eggs, spinach, naruto slices, pork cutlet slices, and nori leaves over the noodles, distributing them evenly.

 For 4 **MILKSHAKE GLASSES** - Preparation: 5 MIN - LEVEL ✦

Eager to get back to the picnic with Annie and Patty, you decide to make them a fruit drink that will delight them when the time comes.

STRAWBERRY HAPPINESS
STRAWBERRY AND BANANA SMOOTHIE

INGREDIENTS

8 drops orange blossom
1 ½ cup (400 ml) banana
juice
4 tbsp vanilla-flavored yogurt
(p. 179)
8 tbsp whipped cream
3 tbsp (20 g) slivered almonds

FOR THE COULIS
16 strawberries
⅓ cup (60 g) sugar
Juice of 1 lemon
2 tbsp water

EQUIPMENT

Mixer

Prepare the fresh strawberry coulis with care and affection. Begin by rinsing the strawberries, then hull and quarter them. Blend for 1 minute, adding the sugar, lemon juice, and water. Set the coulis aside.

Now bring all your energy to the fruit smoothie. Pour the strawberry coulis, orange blossom, banana juice, and vanilla yogurt into the blender. Blend vigorously for 1 minute and 30 seconds.

Divide the smoothie into 4 milkshake glasses. Adorn your creation with whipped cream and delicately sprinkle flaked almonds on top.

Your delightful drink is now ready to be relished.

PREPARING FOR THE SANCTUARY

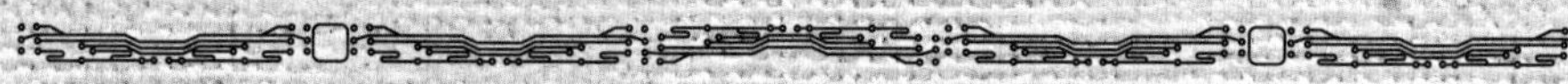

HYOGA SHOT

INGREDIENTS
4 tsp (20 ml) white rum
2 tsp (10 ml) curaçao
2 tsp (10 ml) Cartron Whitemint

THE DIAMOND DUST IS YOURS!

🍀 Begin with the heaviest element: pour the white rum into the shot, followed by the curaçao and Whitemint.

🍀 Savor this creation, but take heed, for its potency should not be underestimated.

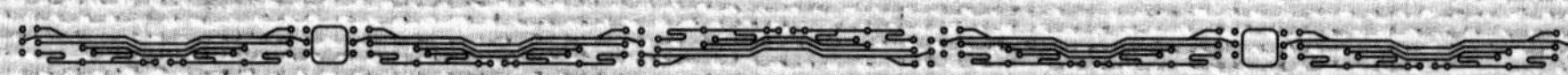

PHOENIX SHOT

INGREDIENTS
4 tsp (20 ml) vodka
2 tsp (10 ml) curaçao
2 tsp (10 ml) kirsch liqueur

From whence do these waves arise? Caution against the Phoenix Illusion!

🍀 Into the shot, pour the vodka, then add the curaçao and kirsch. An ideal means to return from the abyss…

PEGASUS SHOT

INGREDIENTS
4 tsp (20 ml) gin
2 tsp (10 ml) rooibos tea liqueur

BY THE METEORS OF PEGASUS! Pour the gin into the shot, then add the tea liqueur.

Feel the cosmo-energy diffusing from this sacred liquid.

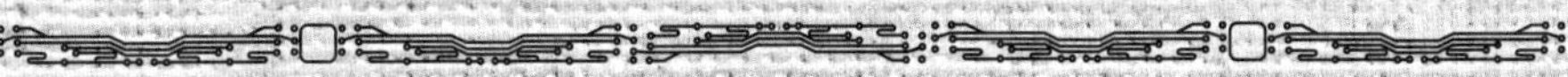

DRAGON SHOT

INGREDIENTS
4 tsp (20 ml) melon liquor
2 tsp (10 ml) white wine
2 tsp (10 ml) Tabasco

Withstand the cosmos shock from the WRATH OF THE DRAGON!

In the shot glass, pour the melon liquor, then add the white wine and the Tabasco.

SHUN SHOT

INGREDIENTS
4 tsp (20 ml) Hendricks gin
2 tsp (10 ml) watermelon syrup

Prepare to face the Nebular Chain...

Pour the gin into the shot, then add the watermelon syrup.

Don't be fooled by its apparent gentleness...

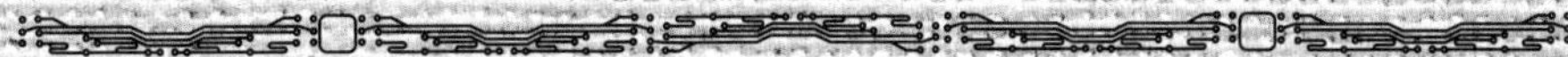

For 1 **TUMBLER GLASS** - Preparation: **5 MIN** - LEVEL ✦ ✦

Ah, the sea air! Judging by your Log Pose, you're well on your way to the next island... What adventure awaits you there? Now that's a good question! Why don't you go and mix yourself a cocktail while you wait?

BINKS NO SALÉ
CAPTAIN MORGAN, TRIPLE SEC, PINEAPPLE AND PASSION FRUIT

INGREDIENTS

4 tsp (20 ml) Angostura Bitter
8 tsp (40 ml) Captain Morgan Spiced
4 tsp (20 ml) triple sec
6 tsp (30 ml) pineapple juice
2 tsp (10 ml) lemon juice
1 pinch ginger powder
½ passion fruit
1 lemon slice
1 orange slice
Crushed ice

Pour the Angostura into a tumbler glass.

Add Captain Morgan Spiced, triple sec, pineapple juice, lemon juice and finish with a pinch of ginger.

Add the crushed ice. Stir with a cocktail spoon.

Decorate with half the passion fruit and slices of lemon and orange.

Special presentation: pour the cocktail into a hollowed-out coconut, garnished with passion fruit, lemon and orange slices. Sip through a straw!

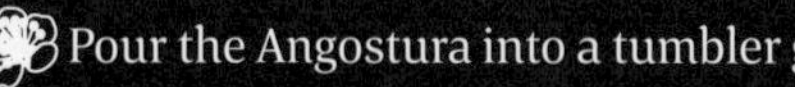

PRINCESS MONONOKE

ROTHS OF VENGEFUL SPIRITS

JAPANESE BROTH, LEEKS AND YUZU

INGREDIENTS

4 pinches dried kikuragé
(black mushrooms)
2 leek whites

2 carrots
8 cups (2 l) sparkling water
1 yuzu

1 tbsp dried bonito dashi
4 cups (1 l) mineral water
2 tsp white miso paste
4 pinches wakame

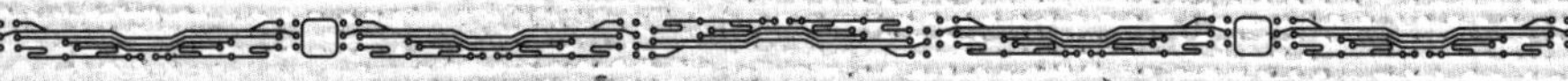

❀ Prepare your vegetables by rehydrating the black mushrooms in a container of water for 20 minutes.

❀ Meanwhile, attend to the leeks and carrots. Rinse the leeks thoroughly and peel the carrots. Use two separate saucepans, each filled with 1 liter of sparkling water, to cook the vegetables à l'anglaise individually.

❀ After cooking, drain and place them in a bowl of iced water to halt the cooking process.

❀ With a chef's knife, finely dice the carrots and set them aside. Cut the leeks into thin strips. Use a zester to sprinkle yuzu zest over the leeks and keep them aside.

❀ Now, let's prepare the broth. Bring 1 liter of mineral water to a boil and add the dried bonito dashi. Reduce the heat and gently stir to blend the dashi.

❀ Take one ladleful of this mixture and combine it with 1 teaspoon of miso paste in a small bowl. Once mixed, pour it back into the saucepan and stir thoroughly. Continue over low heat, adding the remaining miso paste until the broth is ready.

To serve: pour the bonito and miso dashi broth into 4 bowls. Divide the carrots and leeks among the bowls. Sprinkle a pinch of wakame over each bowl and garnish with the rehydrated black mushrooms.

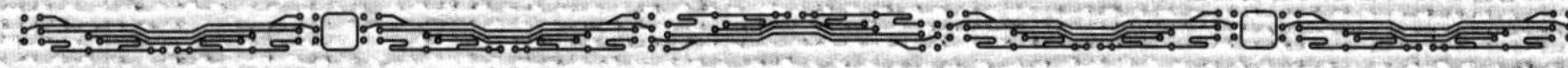

For 1 GLASS - Preparation: 5 MIN - LEVEL ✦

"It is well known among enthusiasts of his work that the great Jules Verne had a certain fondness for Mint Julep, a version all his own. Having had the opportunity to meet him on a trip from London to Paris, here, from memory, is how he wanted me to serve it to him."
Thibaud, bartender for the Canon Train Company

FLY TO THE MOON
MOJITO À LA JULES VERNE

INGREDIENTS

8 mint leaves
2 tsp sugar cocktail
10 tsp (50 ml) cognac
1 cup (250 ml) lemonade
Juice of ½ lemon

6 tsp (30 ml) agricultural rum
1 pinch nutmeg
1 fresh pineapple slice
Crushed ice

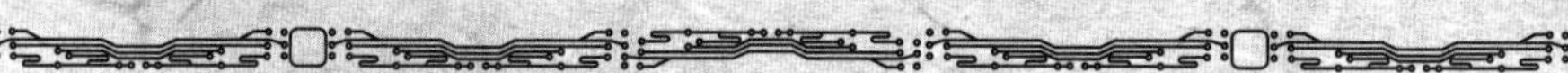

In a julep mug or large metal tumbler, crush 6 mint leaves with 1 teaspoon of cocktail sugar.

Pour in the cognac, add the crushed ice and stir well with your cocktail spoon. Add the lemonade.

Pour in the lemon juice and rum, sprinkle with grated nutmeg and top with a slice of fresh pineapple.

Garnish with the remaining mint.

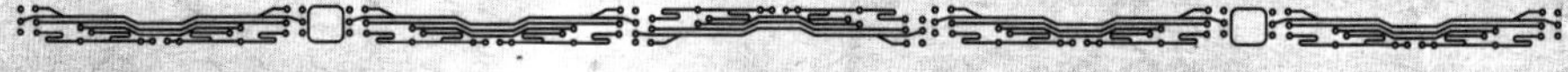

A jewel in the crown of French manga, City Hall is a seinen manga by Rémi Guérin and Guillaume Lapeyre, published by Ankama Éditions since 2012. In a retro-futuristic 20th century, armed with a pen and paper, a talented creator can bring his creature, a Papercut, to life. Imagine London under the attack of a creative villain... The manga's heroes, Jules Verne and Arthur Conan Doyle, will have to fight and stop the evil yet brilliant Lord BlackFowl!

UNAR SCEPTRE

EGG, CAMPARI, GRAPEFRUIT AND TEQUILA

INGREDIENTS

4 tsp (20 ml) lime juice
1 egg white
2 tsp (10 ml) Campari
6 tsp (30 ml) grapefruit juice
4 tsp (20 ml) cane sugar
6 tsp (30 ml) blanco tequila
1 lemon
2 or 3 ice cubes

EQUIPMENT

Boston shaker

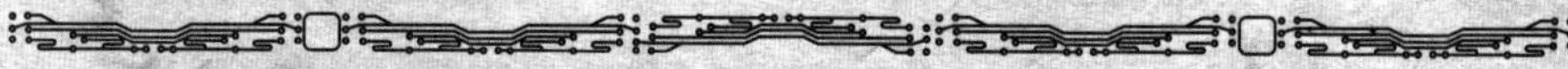

🌸 Pour all the ingredients, except the ice cubes, into the Boston shaker.

🌸 Shake vigorously for 30 seconds to create an emulsion and allow the egg white to foam.

🌸 Pour the ice cubes into the shaker. Shake vigorously again.

🌸 Pour and strain the contents of the Boston shaker into a martini glass.

For **1 OLD FASHIONED GLASS** - Preparation: **5 MIN** - LEVEL ✦ ✦

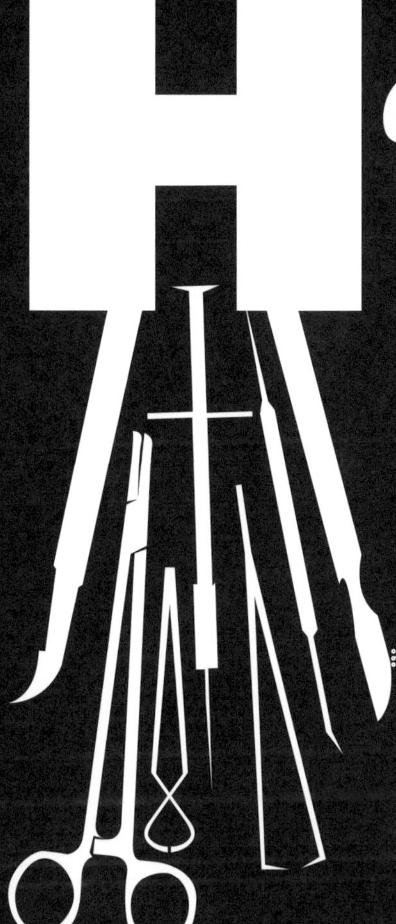

HONMA SPECIAL
TEQUILA, GINSENG LIQUEUR AND TURMERIC

INGREDIENTS

8 tsp (40 ml) tequila
4 tsp (20 ml) Kamm & Sons Ginseng
2 tsp (10 ml) lemon juice
2 tsp (10 ml) cane sugar
1 pinch turmeric
1 tbsp crushed ice

EQUIPMENT

Shaker

❀ Prepare a revitalizing drink by combining tequila, ginseng liqueur, lemon juice, and cane sugar in a shaker. Shake vigorously for 20 seconds, then set the shaker aside briefly.

❀ Create a base of crushed ice in an old-fashioned glass. Pour the contents of the shaker over the ice and sprinkle a pinch of turmeric on top. Enjoy!

In 1973, Osamu Tezuka, known as the "father of manga," applied his medical expertise to craft the adventures of Black Jack. This series follows the story of a brilliant doctor and surgeon who chooses to practice medicine outside the law. Unique in appearance due to a skin graft from a childhood accident, he resembles a Frankenstein-like figure. A recluse, his sole companion is a young girl reconstructed from the organs of a twin who developed inside his sister's body. Through these medical narratives, Tezuka explores the intricacies of the human soul and its darker facets.

A

ANGOSTURA

Bitter made from orange peel.

C

CAMPARI

Red Italian bitter.

CAPTAIN MORGAN SPICED

Spiced dark rum. Hints of vanilla, sweet spices and molasses.

COOKING À L'ANGLAISE

À l'Anglaise is a French expression meaning something cooked "in the English manner." Vegetable cooking technique involving immersion in boiling, highly salted water. It helps to pre-season vegetables.

D

DRIED BONITO DASHI

Dashi is a broth made by infusing konbu seaweed in water. It is usually complemented with dried bonito shavings, bonito being a fish in the tuna family.

DUXELLES

A duxelle is a mince of button mushrooms, shallots and onions, browned in melted butter. By extension, it refers to a specific size of minced vegetable.

K

KAMM & SONS GINSENG

A spirit that's a cross between a bitters, a liqueur and a gin. Its 45 ingredients include ginseng, grapefruit zest and an infusion of manuka honey and gentian.

KIKURAGÉ

White or brown mushroom. Used in Asian cuisine, it is often sold dried. Slightly gelatinous when rehydrated, it accompanies many soups and broths in Chinese and Japanese cuisine.

N

NARUTOMAKI

A steamed fish cake roll used for decoration in Japanese cuisine: it's one of the most colorful elements of ramen and is named after the hero of Masashi Kishimoto's manga.

NORI

Grilled seaweed leaves, traditionally used in Japanese cuisine. They are used to coat rice in maki, for example.

UDON NOODLES

Noodles traditionally used in Japanese cuisine: made from a mixture of wheat flour, water and salt, they are thick and can be eaten hot or cold. There are many ways to prepare and eat them.

Tips

BREWING A SUCCESSFUL MATCHA TEA INFUSION

We're not here to tell you about the tea ceremony during which matcha can be consumed: we're not experts, and we wouldn't want to omit any important elements of this ceremony. We'd just like to draw your attention to this fragrant, bitter green tea, so unique to Japan, and to the ideal way to consume it.

INGREDIENTS FOR 4 TEA BOWLS
¾ cup (200 ml) boiling water for the chasen
1 ⅕ cup (300 ml) mineral water for tea
2 level teaspoons matcha tea

ESSENTIAL EQUIPMENT
Chasen (traditional bamboo whisk)
Chawan (high-sided, flat-bottomed tea bowl)
Chashaku (teaspoon)

• Begin by preparing the chasen (bamboo whisk) by pouring boiling water over its bamboo blades to soften them.

• Next, in a saucepan, bring mineral water to a boil and then set it aside.

• Strain the matcha tea powder through a fine-mesh sieve into 4 bowls, using a rate of 2 grams of tea per bowl or ½ level teaspoon per bowl.

• Pour 80 millilitres of hot water down the sides of each bowl. Utilize the chasen to vigorously stir the tea and water, ensuring that any lumps dissolve and a fine froth forms on the liquid's surface. Your matcha tea is now ready to be enjoyed.

MAKING TONKOTSU BROTH

Tonkotsu broth is an Asian broth made from pork bones, and has become the basic broth for ramen in Hakata. The pork bone marrow, bone collagen and adhering flesh break down and mix with the water. It is this mixture that gives the broth its milky white color. There are many ways to make pork bone soup, some simpler than others, some less time-consuming than others. Here's one of the simplest and quickest.

INGREDIENTS FOR 2 L BROTH
20 cups (5 l) water
44 pounds (1 kg) pork bones, crushed

• Pour 2 liters of cold water into a stewpot and add the pork bones. Bring the mixture to a boil and skim off any impurities. Once the pork bones are blanched, remove them.

• In a pressure cooker, place the blanched bones in 3 liters of salted water. Close the pressure cooker and heat it over medium-low heat, allowing approximately 2 hours from the initial simmering.

• After the time has elapsed, remove the pressure cooker from the heat and carefully release the steam. Open the cooker and strain the resulting juice.

If there's one thing I've learned on my travels, it's that the multiverse is governed by certain immutable rules.

It all began during a peculiar cycle where each stage of my journey unfolded in universes that, while similar, were remarkably distinct. Allow me to continue my tale...

Picture this: I found myself at home in my humble library, sharing a cigar with a new friend who claimed possession of a mysterious artifact granting access to infinite imaginary worlds.

Skeptical, just as you might be, he pulled something from his pocket, gestured, and asked me to select a book from the shelves. A blinding light filled the room, and my adventure began...

Through numerous stopovers, I encountered a succession of illustrated worlds whose logic sometimes eluded me. Roaming through these realms, my perseverance and inherent wit led me to conceive a few 'immutable rules that are essential for surviving a world of heroes suffering from mydriasis'.

1) Every universe has its heroes. They may be good or evil, male or female, but these figures stand out amid the populace, and in particular because:

a. They have names and traits that distinguish them from most of the people who you meet. The lives of the heroes teem with drama, and even their trivial issues eclipse the worst fates of ordinary folks.

b. They are significantly stronger, more beautiful, and overall more remarkable than the rest of the world. You'll see them, and you'll immediately sense that their lives are hectic (and probably fraught with death and suffering).

c. Most heroes never really die and any that do, perish at the end of an event of increasing dramatic intensity uttering something epic and inspiring with their last breath. In comparison, the rest of the population receives little fanfare and recognition when they find themselves at death's door.

2. Great villains meet heroes head-on. Their powers match the heroes', presenting a fair challenge. Imagine Boo confronting Son Goku in the early days, still munching on his boogers! Toriyama's Dragon Ball character, with the tendency to gain strength near death, epitomizes this dynamic.

3. Love's pursuit is fraught with trials. Heroic quests for love entail enduring all hardships before realizing that the cherished other half was nearby all along. It's the tale of Candy by Igarashi and Mizuki, enduring separation, loss, and trials in a quest for love—a narrative pattern in '70s shôjo manga heroines. Not everyone has the same luck in life...

4. Anything is possible. These worlds host beings with delicate necks in ancient trees, leggy schoolgirls with a disturbed astral chart saving the world, and immensely powerful ninjas atop giant frogs—offering dreamlike, psychedelic, or realistic yet never monotonous narratives.

5. Rules have exceptions. Nothing is fixed in these whimsical worlds, rendering all principles subject to variation.

These guidelines showcase the vibrant, ever-evolving, enchanting multiverse. It's a refreshing yet exhausting journey! Occasionally, I join Luffy, Zoro, and Nami —whose father is none other than Eichiro Oda— aboard the Vogue Merry, sailing the Grand Line in search of the elusive One Piece, while enjoying fishing and brief stays, as conflicts often arise wherever we dock.

You'll recognize Princess Mononoke *(Hayao Miyazaki's 1997 animated film),* Sailor Moon *(Naoko Takeuchi's 1992 shôjo), and* Naruto *(Masashi Kishimoto's 1999 manga), respectively!*

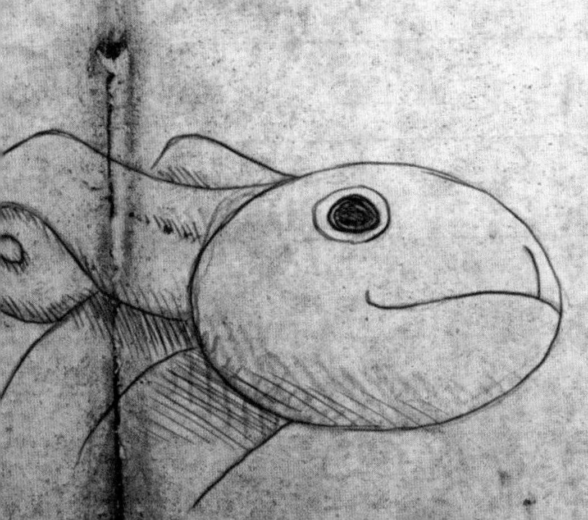

FANTASTIC

For **1 SHOT** - Preparation: **5 MIN** - LEVEL ✦

RAAAAIIIIINNN

BRAIN HEMORRHAGE VARIANT

INGREDIENTS

4 tsp (20 ml) vodka
4 tsp (20 ml) grenadine syrup
2 tsp (10 ml) Bailey's

Ah! It's you again! Did you finally catch your prey? Was he hard to kill? Well, since you've earned it, here's a little treat for a persistent zombie!

🐙 Pour the vodka into the shot.

🐙 Then add the grenadine. Once the grenadine is at the bottom of the glass, get the Bailey's.

🐙 To make sure you get the "brain effect" right, pour the Bailey's onto a teaspoon so that it falls gently into the glass as it overflows from the spoon.

Serves 4 - Preparation: **20 MIN** - Cooking: **40 MIN** - LEVEL ✦ ✦ ✦

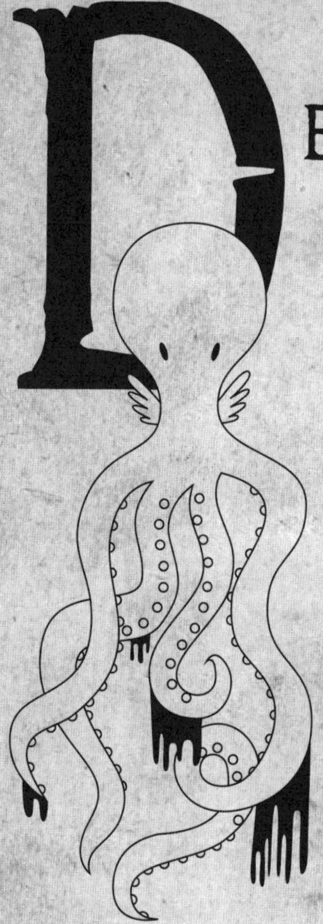

DEEP SMOKED

FUMET OF LANGOUSTINE AND SAFFRON CHANTILLY CREAM

INGREDIENTS

12 langoustines
2 celery stalks
5 shallots
1 onion
1 small carrot
1 bouquet garni
½ cup (150 ml) white
wine

4 cups (1 l) fresh water
1 tsp olive oil
½ bunch fresh
coriander
8 bread croutons
(p. 123)
Espelette pepper
Salt and pepper

FOR THE WHIPPED
CREAM
1 cup (250 ml)
full-fat whipping cream
2 saffron capsules
Salt

EQUIPMENT

Electric whisk
Fine sieve

🐙 Chill a pan and the paddles of an electric whisk in the freezer.

🐙 Start by preparing the fumet. Peel the langoustines, reserving the flesh, and place the heads in a stewpot, discarding the tails and shells.

🐙 Rinse the celery stalks, shallots, onion, and carrot, then chop them into mirepoix.

🐙 Combine the aromatic garnish, bouquet garni, white wine, and fresh water in the stewpot. Simmer over low heat for 40 minutes.

🐙 After 20 minutes, work on the saffron Chantilly cream. Retrieve your chilled equipment and pour the whipping cream into the mixing bowl. Add 2 pinches of salt and the saffron. Whip briskly until the cream thickens, then set it aside in a cool place.

🐙 Heat olive oil in a frying pan over high heat. Sauté the langoustines briefly, then set them aside until serving. Finely chop fresh coriander and set it aside.

🐙 Once the 40 minutes have passed, remove the stewpot from the heat. Strain the stock through a fine sieve, pressing the scampi carcasses against the sieve with a ladle to extract maximum flavor.

Presentation: In each soup plate, place 2 croutons, 3 seared langoustines, and a sprinkle of coriander. Make quenelles with the whipped cream and add one to each plate. Finish by sprinkling a few pinches of Espelette pepper over each quenelle. Finally, pour the fumet into each plate and savor the dish!

"It's not easy to recover from your emotions! Locked in a cold room with a corpse—and with ice cream—interrogated by the whole Fratelli family, tied up with Sinok! All that, and the discovery of Willy le Borgne's treasure! My word, I'm going to need one hell of a pick-me-up..."

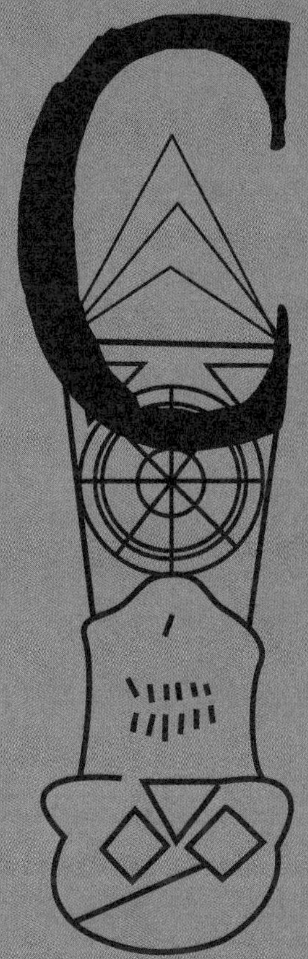

CHUNKSHAKE

VANILLA MILKSHAKE WITH CHOCOLATE AND COOKIE CHIPS, WHIPPED CREAM AND CARAMEL SAUCE

INGREDIENTS

FOR THE CARAMEL SAUCE
⅘ cup (180 g) sugar
5 ⅔ tbsp (80 g) soft butter, cut into pieces
1 ⅓ cup (300 ml) full-fat liquid cream

FOR THE MILKSHAKE
2 cups (500 ml) good quality vanilla ice cream
2 cups (500 ml) whole milk
¼ cup (40 g) dark chocolate chips

FOR TOPPING
Chantilly cream (p. 43)
4 chocolate chip cookies
3 tbsp (20 g) slivered almonds

EQUIPMENT

Blender

🐙 Begin by preparing the caramel sauce. Heat sugar in a frying pan over medium-high heat, stirring continuously. As it begins to brown and liquefy, add the butter pieces. Stir until the mixture melts and the butter blends with the sugar. Gradually add the liquid cream, stirring continuously. Transfer the smooth caramel sauce to a bowl.

🐙 Break the cookies into large pieces and set them aside.

🐙 Now, let's make the vanilla milkshake. In a blender, combine vanilla ice cream and whole milk. Blend at maximum power for 2 minutes. Add 1 teaspoon of caramel sauce and chocolate chips, then blend for an additional 10 seconds.

For garnish: pour the vanilla milkshake into 4 tall glasses. Drizzle a bit of caramel sauce into each glass (reserving some for the Chantilly cream). Generously add the Chantilly cream on top and sprinkle with slivered almonds. Finish by placing cookie pieces on top and pouring over the remaining caramel sauce. Behold, a milkshake worthy of the legendary Lawrence Cohen!

For 1 OLD FASHIONED GLASS - Preparation: **2 MIN** - LEVEL ✦ ✦

"Proud is the McLeod clan at the dawn of the battle against the Fraser clan. Few know all our secrets, but I'm sure this one won't remain in the shadows for long. It's the key to our courage and recklessness. Some would say it will be our undoing. Connor and I keep telling them that it's the secret of our immortality! Tomorrow, we fight these dogs, and I, Dougal, hope to bring honor to my clan. MCLEOD! MCLEOD!"
Translated from Old Scottish Gaelic – text found in the ruins of a Highland village – 1535 A.D.

A strange recipe follows, translated as follows:

GLENN FINAN'S TWISTS AND TURNS

DEWAR'S, DRAMBUIE, ANGOSTURA

INGREDIENTS

8 tsp (40 ml) Dewar's 12-year-old scotch
6 tsp (30 ml) Drambuie
2 dashes Angostura Bitter

Pour the scotch and Drambuie into an old-fashioned glass.

Finish with Angostura Bitter.

For **10 SHOTS OF 2 FL OZ (60 ML)** - Preparation: **20 MIN** - Rest: **3 to 4 H** - LEVEL ✦ ✦ ✦

Exhausted from fighting spectres and other ghostly miasmas? Jaded by the phone call from that old-lady whose fridge also seems to be a doorway to a horrific dimension? Relax and prepare yourself a little pick-me-up worthy of the name!

SLIMER JELLO SHOT

VODKA, GET 27 AND MINT JELLY

INGREDIENTS

1 ½ cup (400 ml) water
6 ⅔ tbsp (100 ml) vodka
6 ⅔ tbsp (100 ml) Get 27
½ cup (100 ml) crème de menthe
1 tbsp (9 g) gelatin powder

EQUIPMENT

1 aerosol cooking grease (or commercially available oil spray)

🐙 Pour 200 millilitres of water, vodka, Get 27 and crème de menthe into a container. Mix well and chill in the fridge for 30 minutes.

🐙 Bring the remaining water to the boil and stir in the powdered gelatin. Remove the saucepan from the heat and stir until the gelatine has dissolved.

🐙 Remove from the fridge and stir into the gelatin mixture. Set aside.

🐙 Now prepare your shot glasses to receive the greenish ectoplasmic liquid you've just made. Using the aerosol, spray the inside of the shot glasses so that the jello can easily slide out later and be easily consumed.

🐙 Pour the mixture into the glasses and place your shots in the fridge for 3 to 4 hours.

🐙 As soon as the contents of the shots have set, gobble them up, and when you see Dr. Venkman, be sure to tell him about the cupcake!

For 1 LOW WHISKY GLASS - Preparation: **5 MIN** - LEVEL ✦

"You're not far from finding the Idol. Your guide, Satipo, will join you this evening at Bar Morris, calle Boza, Lima. Relax and enjoy the local cocktails. You'll have plenty of time to get deep into the jungle tomorrow.
Best regards.
M.B. "

CHACHAPOYAN
ADVENTURE VERSION OF PISCO SOUR

INGREDIENTS

6 ⅔ tbsp (100 ml) pisco
Juice of ½ lime
⅔ tbsp (10 ml) cane sugar syrup
1 egg white
Ground cinnamon
Crushed ice

EQUIPMENT

Shaker

Pour the pisco, lime juice, cane sugar syrup and egg white into a shaker.

Fill the shaker with crushed ice and shake vigorously.

While straining the ice, pour the mixture into a low whisky glass.

Sprinkle the mousse lightly with cinnamon. Enjoy and don't think about tomorrow…

"Here's the recipe for Mamuschka as taught to us by our Cossack cousins: we tasted it during the burning of Rome, we tasted it at Waterloo, we tasted it for Jack the Ripper. Doesn't that ring a bell?"

The MAMUSCHKA

CHOCOLATE CREAM, COGNAC AND LICOR 43

INGREDIENTS

4 tsp (20 ml) Fee Brothers Aztec Chocolate Bitters
4 tbsp (60 ml) cognac Hine
4 tsp (20 ml) Licor 43
1 vanilla pod
Crushed ice

EQUIPMENT

Mixing glass
Cocktail spoon
Julep filter

Voluptuously pour the Bitters into a mixing glass, followed by 20 ml of cognac and Licor 43.

Add crushed ice to half the glass and stir with the cocktail spoon.

Add 20 ml of cognac and crushed ice up to ⅔ of the glass, and stir again. Add the rest of the cognac and another dose of crushed ice, and stir again.

Pour the mixture into a martini glass, straining with a julep filter.

Don't forget to garnish this Brotherly Love cocktail with a vanilla pod…

Originally a TV series in the 1960s created by David Levi and based on the characters imagined by Charles Addams, *The Addams Family* has been adapted several times for film, television and even as a musical. Its best-known version is Barry Sonnenfeld's 1991 film, starring Raúl Juliá, Christopher Lloyd and Anjelica Huston. *The Addams Family*, with its dark humor and madcap quality, is one of those rare gothic works that is so popular with the general public, a feat usually achieved by the master Tim Burton.

For **4 CUPS** - Preparation: **5 MIN** - Cooking: **10 MIN** - LEVEL ✦ ✦

VIN FIERT

MULLED WINE WITH VODKA AND RED FRUIT

INGREDIENTS

4 cups (1 l) red wine
1 tbsp honey
5 cloves
1 cinnamon stick
¼ cup (50 g) strawberries, washed and hulled
⅓ cup (50 g) raspberries
4 tsp (20 ml) lemon juice
⅓ cup (80 ml) vodka

EQUIPMENT

Hand Blender
Strainer

🐙 Pour the wine, honey, cloves, cinnamon, fruit and lemon juice into a saucepan.

🐙 Heat over medium-high heat for 10 minutes, stirring constantly.

🐙 Leave the pan on the heat, remove the cinnamon stick and, using an immersion blender, blend for 30 seconds.

🐙 Strain the mixture, then pour the clear juice into 4 cups.

🐙 Pour 20 ml of vodka into each cup and enjoy.

For **1 GLASS** - Preparation: **15 MIN** - LEVEL ✦ ✦ ✦

"Watch out, lads, 'cause this stuff's got a kick! Ectoplasm be damned! Now that's the kind of stuff you'll want to try to get up the courage to get those bastards out of your house! Introduction to recipe 6121 of the Guide for the Recently Deceased."

EXPERIMENT N°6121

ESPRESSO, WHITE DOG RYE WHISKEY AND TIA MARIA

INGREDIENTS

2 tbsp (30 ml) espresso coffee
4 tbsp (60 ml) Buffalo Trace White Dog rye whiskey
4 tsp (20 ml) Tia Maria
1 tsp honey
3 tbsp dry ice (p. 123)

EQUIPMENT

Shaker

🐙 Prepare the espresso coffee, either using the good old plunger coffee maker technique, or by using an espresso machine.

🐙 Once your coffee has cooled completely, pour it with the rest of the ingredients into a shaker. Shake briskly to create the emulsion.

🐙 Pour into a chemist's flask or balloon glass to maintain good oxygenation of the liquid.

To serve: place the balloon in a larger container ⅓ filled with dry ice (p. 123). Pour a little water over the dry ice to generate smoke. Be careful with dry ice, kid: even in death, you're risking a lot playing with this stuff. Be sure to read the instructions in the tips section of this book.

250
APPROX
200
15

For 1 TULIP GLASS - Preparation: 5 MIN - LEVEL ✦ ✦

You're ready to set off in search of your truck and Wang's girlfriend, of course! You just don't want to run out of energy for the fight ahead against that pesky Lo Pan! Here's a little specialty straight from EggShen's cabinet.

SHEN TONIC

NIGORI YUZUSHU AND CITRUS COCKTAIL

INGREDIENTS

4 tbsp (60 ml) Nigori Yuzushu 12.5
4 tsp (20 ml) yuzu juice
6 ⅔ tbsp (100 ml) orange juice
1 cocktail spoon grenadine syrup
1 ripe kumquat
2 tsp crushed ice

EQUIPMENT

Cocktail spoon

Pour the Nigori Yuzushu, yuzu juice, orange juice and grenadine syrup into the tulip glass.

Add 1 teaspoon of crushed ice.

Stir briskly with a cocktail spoon.

Finally, add the remaining crushed ice and place the kumquat on the glass. Enjoy!

Big Trouble in Little China is a humorous fantasy adventure film released in 1986 and directed by the master of horror and the bizarre, John Carpenter. Set in San Francisco's Chinatown, the film propels philosophic truck driver Jack Burton, played by Kurt Russell, into the clutches of Chinese sorcerer Lo Pan. To recover Miao Yin and Gracie Law, kidnapped by the Lords of Death, Jack Burton and Wang plunge into the depths of Chinatown and stop at nothing to save their sweethearts. So if you too were ready in the womb, don't miss the fabulous adventures of Jack Burton in the clutches of the Lords of Death.

FANTASTIC
Lexicon

B

BAILEY'S
Irish whiskey, crème fraîche and chocolate liqueur.

D

DRAMBUIE
Scotch liqueur containing Scotch whisky, honey and herbs.

F

FUMET
It is defined as much by the aroma that emerges from a preparation as by a clear, reduced broth.

L

LICOR 43
A liqueur of Spanish origin with 43 secret ingredients.

M

MIREPOIX
Cutting vegetables into 1.5 cm cubes.

P

PISCO
Brandy from Peru and Chile.

S

SCOTCH
Blend of grain and malt whisky made exclusively in Scotland.

Tips

MAKING YOUR OWN BREAD CROUTONS

INGREDIENTS FOR 200 G CROUTONS
3 cups (200 g) farmhouse, sandwich or sourdough bread,
preferably a little dry and cut into thick slices
2 tbsp (30 g) butter or 2 tsp olive oil

• Preheat the oven to 200°C (gas mark 6-7).

• Cut the bread slices into even 1 cm cubes.

• In a frying pan over medium-high heat, melt the butter or heat the olive oil. Add the bread cubes and sauté until they achieve a delightful color. Remove from heat.

• Place the sautéed bread cubes on a baking paper-lined ovenproof tray and bake for approximately 10 minutes.

• Ensure the bread cubes are dried in the oven without burning. Once dried and golden, remove them and set aside.

• Tip: For garlic croutons, follow the same preparation method, but before dicing the bread slices, rub them with a clove of garlic. Then fry them in the fat.

MAKING ICE CREAM OR FROMAGE FRAIS QUENELLES

Making ice cream or fromage frais quenelles requires a material that's neither too firm nor too melting.

• Use two tablespoons to scoop out the cream you wish to dress.

• Use the second spoon to smooth and shape the desired quenelle.

• Ensure the edges of the quenelle are even and smooth.

USING DRY ICE:

Dry ice is solidified carbon dioxide, creating quite a spectacle. However, handling it requires caution.

HERE ARE SOME RULES TO FOLLOW

• Avoid handling dry ice with bare hands due to its −78°C temperature, which can cause blisters or burns. Always wear gloves and preferably handle the ice using tongs or a spoon. Safety goggles are also recommended for protection against splashing.

• Only handle dry ice with care, and children should not use it.

• Store dry ice exclusively in special containers.

• For a cocktail served at room temperature, use a 2 cm-long stick of dry ice, chilling your drink in less than a minute.

• The smoke from dry ice is not toxic, but the residue left in the glass is. Do not consume what remains of the dry ice at the bottom of your glass.

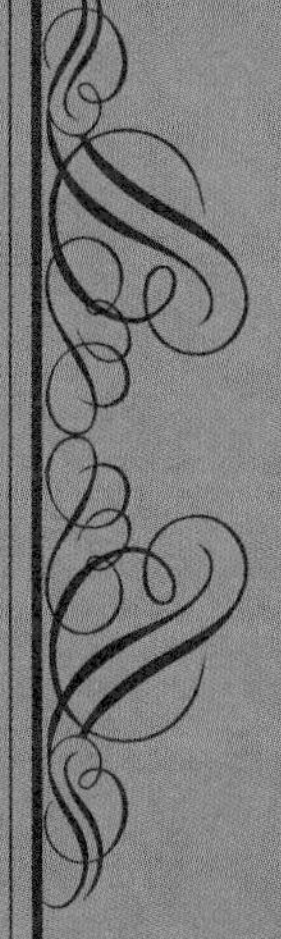

Some of you will already have wondered about the veracity of what you read in this notebook, because it's so hard to believe that travel between Worlds is scientifically possible.

I won't insult you by quoting Clarke's Third Law, but if you want to read on, and follow the story of my journeys, you'll have to accept that, from time to time, it's essential to give up trying to understand and let your imagination take control. And it makes for great stories (and sometimes for interesting profit, albeit too insignificant for any tax officials reading this to care).

I could tell you hundreds of fantastic stories, where mystery and the inexplicable have always aroused human curiosity. But for the derisory price you paid for my precious collection of notes, I'm willing to share a handful of them with you. What all these stories have in common is that they can be told over a drink.

One journey led me to Earth in the 1930s, alongside a tiger trainer posing as an archaeologist. He regaled me with stories while we emptied a bottle, discussing how eternal life had eluded him. You may recognize the adventurous Indiana Jones, whose cinematic escapades left many mysteries unsolved. After all, the Holy Grail wasn't destroyed, so who knows if someone might have got their hands on it after all?

In my quest for immortality, I visited Vlad the Impaler, better known as Count Dracula. He detailed the trivialities of non-life and the eternal frustration of his dietary restrictions. However, his insights into eternal life didn't extend beyond minimal sun protection.

Continuing my exploration, I encountered the putrefied walkers in George A. Romero's *Night of the Living Dead*. While not very communicative, I gathered from their grunts that their secret to longevity was consuming brain juice—an unappetizing regimen.

I needed an immortal who was less... dead. The liveliest of them all had to be from the McLeod clan, a first clan of fighters established deep in the Scottish Highlands. I went to the first part of his adventures, in my opinion the only part worth looking into the career of Connor McLeod, known as 'the Highlander', and asked him about the hundreds of years he had seen defied. His eyes misted over at the mention of the people torn from him by the cruel passage of time. He seemed very lonely to me, but I didn't have time to pour him another glass of (absolutely delicious) whisky before a monster of scarred muscle interrupted our conversation. Wishing to keep my head on my shoulders, literally speaking, I slipped away without asking for a second, but not without taking the bottle of whisky with me (which I still treasure to this day as a precious treat).

The undead mourn and the eternally living are tormented. What a sad picture for a life without finality! So where can I turn for a more cheerful glimpse of eternal life? Bettlejuice, of course!

He's not quite immortal, you might say, but he's probably got the most relevant approach. He escapes death by... continuing to live! Well, it's a life full of flies and mothballs, but he seemed to enjoy himself. He even managed to make a career out of exorcising the 'living'.

Beetlejuice really symbolises the motto 'death really is worth living for'.

That said, I wouldn't recommend his company if you can do without it; in the short time we've been talking, he's managed to belch 18 times (two of which have been insect-filled), spit out a rainbow of sordid colors and 'borrow' eight cigarettes from me, even though I don't even smoke! So I left my exorcist friend Bee… (phew!) and hurried off for a shower.

For the sake of triviality, and because I was a bit peckish (and combining the two seemed like a good idea at the time), I paid a visit to Slimer, the famous ectoplasmic mass of the Ghostbusters. So, dear reader, two important things for you to note:

- Firstly, even his capacity or passion in eating might seem suitable to you as a food companion, Slimer is not the person to go and see for a quick bite to eat. On the contrary, his outrageous way of gobbling up the meal, the cutlery and the table will spoil your appetite;

- Secondly, there are hints that this character's life is rich and full of fascinating stories (there's even a rumor that he was a king a long time ago), but it's absolutely impossible to get anything intelligible out of a conversation with him. The most you'll come away with is a surprising amount of nauseating slime.

Back to reality! I halted my quest for immortality but felt an eerie sensation of being watched. Books by H.P. Lovecraft kept appearing on my desk, hinting at the need to be read or explored. It was a bewildering notion, perhaps a consequence of my extensive travels melding reality and fantasy.

If you're still intrigued by means of defying time's toll, I know an expensive method. Contact me if you're still keen.

If you're interested in a good time, I'd recommend a trip to Astoria in Richard Donner's 1985 film *The Goonies*. Ask for Lawrence Cohen, nicknamed Choco, and don't hesitate to share a pot of ice cream with him, he always has a good story to tell.

I beg your pardon? Shall we get down to business? Yes, of course!

Anyway, I decided to leave my research into immortality at that. Shortly afterwards, however, I was seized by a slight, albeit omnipresent, feeling of being watched and stalked. I realised that certain books were being left open on my desk for no reason. On closer inspection, I realised that they were all works by H.P. Lovecraft. I had the feeling that these works wanted to be read, to be… visited.

But I refused to believe it. I must have travelled too much, and I was probably beginning to confuse the worlds of my travels with reality.

Yet, my dear reader, this impression never left me. Worse still, it came to occupy my nightmares and, as I dreamt of dark tentacular shapes at night, I heard, in my tormented days, distant voices promising me the immortality I had so long sought.

Confusion grew within me and I came to believe I was mad as a hatter. I took the bull by the horns and started researching this evil cult of Cthulhu, and I soon found out what it was all about! Even today, as I write these lines, this unhealthy presence remains, looking over my shoulder and whispering in my ear dark promises of a life without end, as long as I agree to live with millions of hectolitres of salty, fishy water over my head. Understand my hesitation.

Dear traveller,

I heard about your recent research into ways of preventing time from leaving its mark on your face and body. I know a way of doing this, though it is expensive.

Contact me if you are still interested.

Yours sincerely,
Dorian Gray

COMICS

Fender
INRI
BUSH
3271
CASSETTE
PLAYER
STEREO

FORTRESS OF SOLITUDE
Gin, Get 31, curaçao

INGREDIENTS

8 tsp (40 ml) gin
2 tsp (10 ml) grenadine syrup
4 tsp (20 ml) triple sec
6 tsp (30 ml) Get 31
4 tsp (20 ml) curaçao
10 tbsp (150 ml) sparkling water
2 ice cubes

EQUIPMENT

Shot
Shaker

◆ Pour the gin and grenadine syrup into a shot.

◆ Place the shot in a small saucepan filled with water and heat in a bain-marie over low heat for 4 minutes.

◆ Hold the shot in one hand and invert the long-drink glass over it. Keep the shot at the bottom of the long drink and turn it upside down. This way, the shot will be upside down at the bottom of the long drink. Set aside.

◆ Pour the triple sec, Get 31, curaçao and ice cubes into a shaker. Shake briskly for 30 seconds.

◆ While straining the ice cubes, pour the contents of the shaker into the long drink, then top up with sparkling water. By tilting the glass as you drink, the shot will rise slightly, slowly releasing the warmth of the gin and grenadine.

Your Fortress of Solitude is ready, feel its freshness, feel the burning rays of the Earth's Sun...

Inside memo:
Dear Alfred,
Here's the recipe for a little decoction straight from the labs of Wayne Enterprises.
Put them to good use.
L. F.

THE DARK KNIGHT
Eristoff Black vodka, Grey Goose vodka and dry Noilly Prat

INGREDIENTS

2 cups (500 ml) rapeseed oil
  10 tsp (50 ml) Eristoff Black vodka
  ⅓ tsp (1 g) agar-agar
4 tsp (20 ml) Grey Goose vodka
2 tsp (10 ml) dry Noilly Prat
6 ice cubes

EQUIPMENT

Pipette or syringe
Mixing glass
Cocktail spoon
Julep filter
Mini bartender's ladle

◆ Chill rapeseed oil in the refrigerator for 2 hours beforehand.

◆ Pour Eristoff Black into a saucepan and heat it over low heat. Add agar-agar and whisk gently to combine, avoiding excessive air incorporation. Bring it to a boil for 2 to 3 minutes while stirring constantly. Remove it from heat and let it cool for 5 minutes.

◆ Take out the rapeseed oil from the fridge and pour it into a bowl. Then, using a pipette or syringe, drip your Black vodka mixture drop by drop into the bowl. Collect the beads with a sieve and rinse them with clean water. Set them aside.

◆ Place your martini glass in the freezer.

◆ Pour Grey Goose vodka into a mixing glass, followed by Noilly Prat using a cocktail spoon. Add ice cubes up to ⅔ of the glass's height and stir to chill the drink. Add more ice and stir again.

◆ Pour the mixture into your martini glass, straining the ice with a julep filter. The final delicate step is to place the Black vodka beads at the glass's bottom using a mini bartender's ladle.

PENNYWORTH'S VICHYSSOISE
Glazed leek and potato soup

INGREDIENTS

2 cups (200 g) leek whites
2 ¼ tbsp (20 g) celery stalks
½ pound (200 g) Agria potatoes
1 bunch chives
2 ¾ tbsp (40 g) butter
4 cups (1 l) cold water
1 tsp (4 g) salt
1 cup (250 ml) whipping cream
½ cup (100 g) cream cheese
4 pinches pepper

EQUIPMENT

Hand blender
Strainer

Prepare the vegetables by cleaning the leeks and celery. Peel the celery and potatoes.

Cut the leeks and celery à la paysanne and dice the potatoes into a large brunoise. Chop the chives and set them aside.

Melt the butter in a saucepan over low heat, then add the leeks and celery. Sweat the vegetables in the butter for 4 minutes before adding the potato cubes. Mix and moisten with cold water. Season with salt and cook over medium heat for 30 minutes.

Remove the saucepan from the heat. Blend the contents of the pan with an immersion blender and let it cool to room temperature. Add the whipping cream, mixing it well. Strain and chill the mixture.

For presentation: pour the vichyssoise into 4 soup plates. Place a quenelle of fromage frais (p. 123) on each plate, sprinkle with a pinch of black pepper and chives. You can also add a few bread croutons (p. 123) made beforehand.

For **1 GLASS** (Around 330 ml) - Preparation: **5 MIN** - LEVEL ✦ ✦

"If you ask me, this stuff makes you blind, but that's all that Johnny Con-Job bastard wanted to drink before he went on stage. Maybe that's his secret, eh?"
Bob, bartender at CNC, Newcastle

MUCOUS MEMBRANE
Variation of Snakebite served at Casa Nova Club in Newcastle

INGREDIENTS

½ cup (120 ml) Delirium Tremens beer
½ cup (120 ml) chilled demi-sec cider
4 tsp (20 ml) whisky

◆ Pour the Delirium Tremens beer into a glass, then add the cider slowly until fully incorporated.

◆ Add the whisky. Don't drink it all in one go, eh?

Note from B.P.R.D.: The dosage of rations supplied to Agent Rouge is very precise. Nevertheless, in the event of a difficult return from a mission, we advise all our agents to know how to prepare this mixture. They should be able to take it to their quarters at any time.

CODE NAME RED
Bloody Mary revisited

INGREDIENTS

2 tbsp (30 ml) tomato juice
2 tbsp (30 ml) Absolut Pepper vodka
2 drops Tabasco
2 cups (500 ml) amber beer (barley wine)
2 pinches ground ginger

◆ Pour the tomato juice, vodka, and Tabasco into a shot glass.

◆ Be cautious: Hellboy isn't known for his indulgence. Fill a pint glass with amber ale and sprinkle the foam with ground ginger.

Ensure that Hellboy swallows the shooter first before tasting the pint of beer – he'll appreciate it even more. Good luck with that!

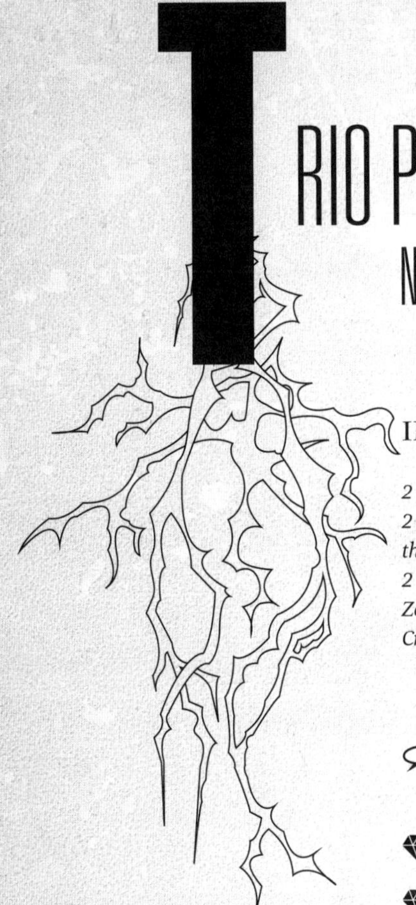

TRIO PALATIN
Negroni Nordic style

INGREDIENTS

2 tbsp (30 ml) aquavit
2 tbsp (30 ml) Antica Formula (Italian liquor,
the king of Vermouth)
2 tbsp (30 ml) Campari
Zest of 1 lemon
Crushed ice

EQUIPMENT

Mixing glass
Julep filter

◆ Pour aquavit, Antica Formula and Campari into a mixing glass with crushed ice.

◆ Stir until cool.

◆ Pour into an old-fashioned glass and strain through a julep filter. Garnish with lemon zest.

GALACTIC MIX

GROOOOT

INGREDIENTS

For 1 TUMBLER GLASS
2 tsp matcha tea (p. 97)
6 ⅔ tbsp (100 ml) fresh water
4 tsp (20 ml) cane sugar syrup
Juice of 1 lime

4 tsp (20 ml) whisky
A few mint leaves
1 stick licorice
2 ice cubes

EQUIPMENT

Shaker
Emulsifier

◆ Pour the matcha and fresh water into a shaker. Use an emulsifier to blend the water and tea for 1 minute, ensuring a seamless mixture and a slight froth on the surface.

◆ Add the cane sugar syrup and lemon juice, then stir for 10 seconds.

◆ Include ice cubes and vigorously shake to cool the tea. After straining the ice cubes, pour the contents of the shaker into a tumbler glass. Add the whisky.

◆ Lastly, lightly tap a few mint leaves onto the rim of the tumbler glass to release their aromas. Garnish the glass with a few mint leaves and a licorice stick.

◆ Enjoy the drink and embrace your inner Groot!

CHARLIE 27

INGREDIENTS

For 1 SHOT
4 tsp (20 ml) limoncello
4 tsp (20 ml) crémant

◆ Pour the limoncello into the shot, then add the crémant.

MARTINEX T'NAGA

INGREDIENTS

For 1 SHOT

4 tsp (20 ml) strawberry liqueur
4 tsp (20 ml) cognac

 Pour the liqueur into the shot, then add the cognac.

STARSHOT

INGREDIENTS

For 1 SHOT

4 tsp (20 ml) triple sec
4 tsp (20 ml) Bols yoghurt liqueur
A few curaçao balls (p. 43)

 Pour the triple sec into the shot, then add the liqueur and curaçao balls!

YONDU UDONTA

INGREDIENTS

For 1 SHOT

4 tsp (20 ml) Hpnotiq vodka
4 tsp (20 ml) curaçao

 Pour Hpnotiq vodka into the shot, then add the curaçao.

STEREO
CASSETTE
PLAYER
BUSH
3271

For **4 GLASSES** - Preparation: **10 MIN** - LEVEL ✦

HAPPY AVOCADO VEGAN REFRESHMENT
Avocado, banana and coconut smoothie

INGREDIENTS

1 ripe avocado
Juice of ½ lemon
1 banana
1 ⅔ cup (400 ml) coconut cream
10 tbsp (150 ml) fresh water
2 tsp sugar
4 large ice cubes

EQUIPMENT

Blender

◆ Making this smoothie couldn't be easier! Begin by preparing the avocado. Slice, pit, and remove the core of the avocado. Transfer the pulp to a blender, incorporating lemon juice to prevent oxidation, and blend briefly.

◆ Next, peel the banana, cut it into sizable chunks, and add it to the blended avocado.

◆ Include the coconut cream, fresh water, sugar, and ice cubes. Blend vigorously for 3 minutes.

◆ Serve the smoothie in 4 tall glasses and relish its refreshing chilliness!

COMIC AWARENESS
Pulque, mezcal and lime

INGREDIENTS

4 tsp (20 ml) pulque
8 tsp (40 ml) mezcal
4 tbsp (60 ml) grapefruit juice
2 tsp (10 ml) lime juice
1 tsp agave syrup
1 tbsp crushed ice
Zest of 1 lemon
1 large cube-shaped ice cube

EQUIPMENT

Shaker

◈ Pour pulque, mezcal, grapefruit juice, lime, agave syrup, and crushed ice into a shaker. Shake vigorously for 15 seconds. Set the shaker aside briefly.

◈ Put a cube-shaped ice cube into an old-fashioned glass.

◈ Pour the contents of the shaker over the ice. Garnish the glass with lemon zest and enjoy!

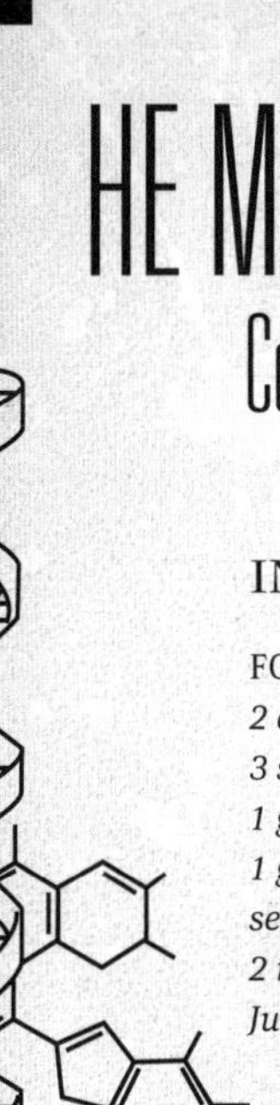

THE MASTODON

Cold cucumber, green bell pepper, avocado and piquillo mousse soup

INGREDIENTS

FOR VEGETABLE JUICE
2 cucumbers
3 spring onions
1 garlic clove
1 green bell pepper, peeled and seeded (p. 152)
2 ripe avocados
Juice of 1 lemon

2 tbsp olive oil
2 tsp sherry vinegar
Salt and pepper

FOR THE PIQUILLO MOUSSE
1 ¾ cup (250 g) peeled and cored piquillos
1 red pepper, seeded
⅘ cup (100 g) fresh goat's cheese

1 cup (250 ml) full-fat whipping cream
Espelette pepper
Salt and pepper

EQUIPMENT

Blender

◆ Experiment 1: Energizing green vegetable juice. Code name: Mastodon.

◆ Prepare your vegetables by peeling and seeding the cucumbers and onions. Cut them into large chunks and set them aside. Peel and seed the garlic, then crush it and set it aside. Cut the green bell pepper into large chunks.

◆ Place everything in a blender and blend vigorously, as if they're being pulverized by the hands of a giant, muscular, green, and very angry entity. Let the mixture sit in the blender for a few moments.

◆ Halve and pit the avocados, then scoop out the cores using a teaspoon. Blend them in a blender along with lemon juice (to prevent darkening), olive oil, sherry vinegar, 2 pinches of salt, and 2 pinches of pepper. Blend again until a fine mousse forms. Chill the mixture in the fridge and serve it chilled!

◆ Experiment 2: Piquillo and Espelette pepper mousse. Lab note: an additional step to infuse a hint of spice into this invigorating potion.

◆ In a blender, combine the piquillos, red pepper, fresh goat's cheese, and crème fleurette until the surface becomes frothy. Season to taste with salt and pepper and then chill the mixture in the fridge.

To serve: pour the cold soup into 4 tall glasses. Then, using a teaspoon, delicately spoon the mousse over the soup. Sprinkle it lightly with Espelette pepper. Now, savor the drink and feel the energy invigorating your muscles. But there's no need to smash the glasses on the floor...

A

AQUAVIT

From the Latin aqua et vitae, literally "brandy", aquavit is a cereal or potato brandy, usually flavored with aromatic herbs. It's a traditional Scandinavian drink.

B

BITTER (COCKTAIL)

A bitter-sweet blend of aromatic herbs and plant peel.

BLANCH

A technique used to tenderize a food or remove its pungency by placing it in a boiling water bath for a few moments, then plunging it into an ice water bath to stop the cooking process.

BLEND

Whisky blending, for example, involves blending several whiskies from different distilleries to create a single whisky.

BOURBON

American whiskey made from a mixture of malted cereals, barley and rye.

BROWN

Cooking food in a little fat over high heat until golden brown.

C

COCKTAIL SPOON

Also known as a mixing spoon. A spoon used to stir the various elements of a cocktail into a mixing glass.

COCKTAIL STRAINER

A strainer is used to filter the solid contents of a cocktail to retain only the liquid.

COOKING IN A BAIN-MARIE

Placing a container holding a preparation in a bath of boiling water to cook or reheat it.

D

DEGERMINATE GARLIC

As garlic is generally difficult to digest, it's best to remove the germ from the clove. Peel a clove and cut it in half, then, using the tip of a knife, remove the germ, the firmer, slightly green comma-shaped part.

DEGLAZE

The process of dissolving and recovering the substances (cooking juices) attached to the bottom of a pan or dish using a liquid added at the end of cooking, such as water, wine, liquid cream, etc.

F

FINELY CHOP

Using a knife to cut vegetables or herbs into small pieces or thin strips.

G

GET

Spearmint or mint liqueur at 21° or 27° respectively.

GT AGRIA

A versatile potato suitable for all types of cooking.

H

HAND BLENDER

The hand blender is highly convenient for making cream, velouté, or soup directly in the saucepan or salad bowl: its sharp blades can effortlessly transform vegetables into a smooth soup or purée. Always ensure the blade is directed towards the bottom of the container to prevent splashing.

If you wish to incorporate more air into your preparation, angle the hand blender at 45° towards the bottom of the container. This technique allows air to infuse the mixture, resulting in a lighter, frothier texture more effortlessly.

P

PAYSANNE

Vegetables cut into 1 to 2cm cubes, to be then cut again into thin slices.

POACH

Cooking food in a simmering liquid.

R

REDUCE

Reducing the volume of a sauce, stock or juice by letting the preparation cook at a low boil to generate evaporation. Reducing to glaze: consists in reducing the volume of a preparation until its texture is syrupy.

ROUX

A mixture of melted butter and flour.

RUM

Brandy produced by fermenting and then distilling sugarcane.

S

SHAKE

Mix vigorously using a shaker.

SIMMER

Cooking food slowly over low heat.

STEW

Cooking slowly over low heat, covered, until the consistency of compote is obtained.

STOUT

A top-fermented beer, very dark in color and recognizable by its bitterness. Guinness is a stout.

SWEAT

Cooking vegetables over low heat to release flavors without adding color. Shake vigorously with a shaker.

T

THIN DOWN

In cooking, as in cocktails, thining down a liquid means diluting it slightly with another liquid.

V

VICHYSSOISE

A classic of French gastronomy, vichyssoise is a vegetable soup.

W

WHISKY

Brandy obtained from barley, corn, rye or cereals.

PEEL PEPPERS (INDIGESTIBLE SKIN)

The bell pepper is a fruit often cooked as a vegetable. Originating from Central and South America and boasting high levels of vitamin C, fiber, and water content, it distinguishes itself from chili peppers by its larger size and lack of spiciness! However, its skin can be indigestible for those with sensitive stomachs. Here are two methods to remove the skin from peppers, making them more digestible in salads, creams, veloutés, etc.

IN THE OVEN:

• Preheat the oven to 200°C (Gas mark 6-7).

• Place the peppers on a baking sheet lined with foil and bake for 20 minutes.

• Once the skin has blackened, take the peppers out of the oven and seal them in a plastic food bag or another sheet of aluminum foil for a few minutes.

• With the condensation, the skin will be easy to remove. Proceed to remove the seeds and prepare the pepper for use in salads or creams.

STEMMING THE BELL PEPPER:

Similar to tomatoes, use the tip of a knife to cut a cross into the top of the bell pepper. Submerge it in a pot of boiling water for 2 minutes, then transfer it to a bowl of cold water. The skin will peel off easily.

OVEN TEMPERATURES

Gas mark 1	30°C - 59°C
Gas mark 2	60°C - 89°C
Gas mark 3	90°C - 119°C
Gas mark 4	120°C - 149°C
Gas mark 5	150°C - 179°C
Gas mark 6	180°C - 209°C
Gas mark 7	210°C - 239°C
Gas mark 8	240°C - 269°C

INFUSING SPICES IN A LIQUID

Infusion involves releasing the aromas into a boiling liquid, which is then allowed to cool.

In cooking, you can infuse hay or vanilla in milk, for example.

EXAMPLE: CINNAMON-FLAVORED APPLE JUICE

INGREDIENTS FOR AN APPLE-CINNAMON MIXTURE
1 l apple juice
2 cinnamon sticks

• Pour the apple juice and cinnamon sticks into a saucepan. Bring to the boil and remove from the heat.

• Leave the cinnamon to infuse for 10 minutes before straining the liquid. You now have apple juice with cinnamon accents.

Believe it or not, dear reader, I discovered comics late in life. By which I mean that this form of storytelling didn't fall into my hands until an advanced age. So please forgive in advance any disillusioned (read: cynical) remarks I may unwillingly blurt out in these lines.

In this chapter, I'd like to introduce you to some of my favorite heroes. Of course, not all of them have my preference for the same reasons, and some are as admirable symbols of justice as they are execrable tavern mates, but I have fond memories of the times I've spent in their company.

I couldn't begin without talking about Superman, the figurehead of the DC Comics staple created by Jerry Siegel in 1933. That paragon of righteousness, inflexible, infallible, incredibly powerful and deadly dull. Excuse me, Clark, but I have to tell the world how impervious you are to piquant humor, lame jokes and, generally speaking, anything that might trigger the hilarity of a table intoxicated with adulterated beer and bad wine.

Because here's your REAL weakness, Kal, you can't get drunk. And I regret to say that this forever deprives you of the most important quality of a drinking companion: you don't forget what you've been told in the middle of the night, after three bottles and as many shots. From then on, when we wake up the next morning in a painful, guilty haze, your clear eyes judge us and our shameful confessions, and it's unbearable. But it takes one like you, incorruptible and strong, to inspire us. And to get us home safely at the end of the evening, too.

At the other end of the hero spectrum (and only slightly younger, he was created in 1939 and today, like Superman, is part of DC's hero adventures) is Batman. Dark and ingenious, no stranger to vice, he relies more on cunning than on the irresistible power of his strength and wealth (which, in all honesty, is probably the very first of his superpowers). You'd think he wouldn't be laughing much more than our Kryptonian friend. In truth, his sense of humor is so cynical that probably only the Joker understands his jokes. The best of which is undoubtedly the one about leaving this demented, bloodthirsty criminal alive, who makes Arkham prison look like a windmill. If Bruce Wayne were a cocktail, he'd be a vodka... a blend at once icy and acidic, simple and subtle. Such is the elegance of the billionaire who sticks his vengeful fist in your face at dusk, promising you a rude awakening.

The person I'd most recommend accompanying to a sleazy bar in any American metropolis is Hellboy, the famous character created by Mike Mignola. Anung, from his demonic moniker, seems to be the epitome of the saloon-goer. Rather touchy (and I say "rather" so as not to write "inordinately", otherwise I'd probably quickly find myself on the wrong end of his clenched fist [his BIG fist]), quick to anger and endowed with a taste for what might trivially be called "a good fight", he drinks, smokes and swears. What could be better?

Dare I make a comparison with Bruce Banner, The Hulk (created by Jack Kirby and Stan Lee)? Like Hellboy, it's best not to piss him off. All in all, that's what they have in common. And to be perfectly honest, their anger is expressed in quite different proportions. Hellboy, for example, could break the entire furniture of the establishment in which you're sipping your quart of red if you were to make the clumsy mistake of knocking over his glass. Behold the man's self-control. Good. Now, imagine doing the same thing to the Hulk; let's say, on a lucky day, it would ONLY result in the obliteration of half the state. Nonetheless, he remains a warm and teasing companion. Note that I've had a guy tell him a joke in a sleazy bar, just to lighten the mood a bit. Hulk smiled, the guy relaxed slightly. Then Hulk patted him lightly on the shoulder with all the sympathy in the world. But all the sympathy in the world was no match for all the Hulkean strength concentrated in the giant's colossal palm. I hear the guy's just out of hospital...

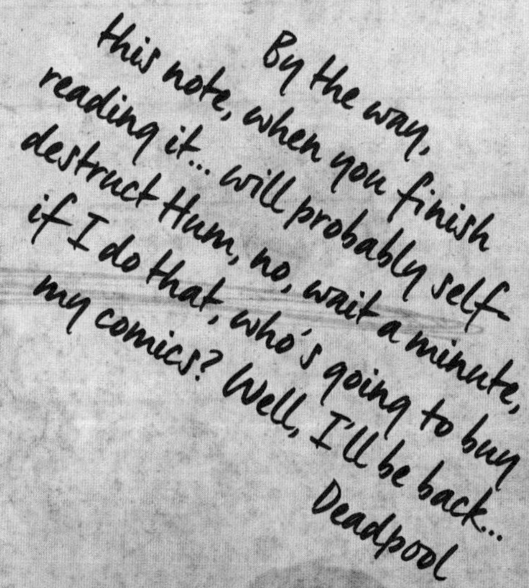

A great team to spend some time in a (galactic) tavern with are the members of the Guardians of the Galaxy (especially those of the 2008 version, which follows on from the 1969 version created by Arnold Drake and Gene Colan); these heroes of the Marvel universe have no equal when it comes to starting a fight, sometimes within their own ranks. My advice: make sure you end up on Drax's side. "The Destroyer isn't just there for show. Oh, and if Gamora gets involved, it's no longer a fight, it's a firing squad (and you're not holding the gun). Flight is the way to go.

A basic list of the 3 superpowers every conscientious world traveller dreams of having

1. Invisibility: We're travellers, and while we'd love to chat with the local protagonists, it's always best to avoid intervening, as this could change the course of events, and we're just observers. Have you ever heard of Super Maximus Wonder Boy? No? That's because on one of my journeys, I clumsily deflected the trajectory of the ray that was supposed to transform him into a superhero. Today, he lives in total anonymity (and I feel terrible about it, especially as this anecdote cost me a lot of money in damages!)

2. The super-memory: There's no need to dwell on this, as forgetting nothing allows you to come back with much better stories. Certain details deserve to be forgotten forever.

3. Teleportation: Useful. But dangerous, depending on how it's activated. I'd like to avoid ending my life stuck in a wall. It's certainly worth the effort.

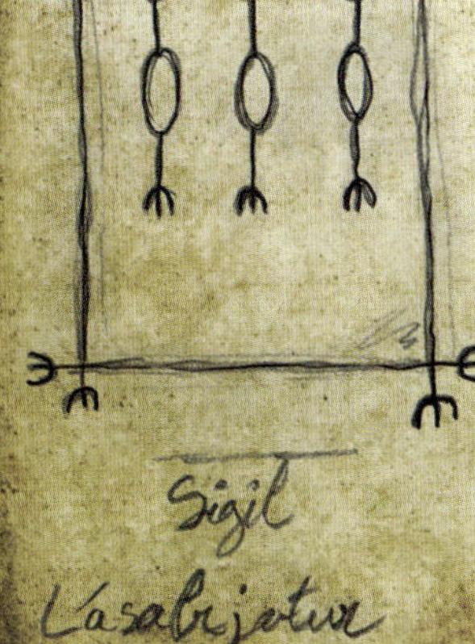

I'll quickly mention Thor (another Marvel hero created by Lee, Kirby and Lieber), who is a fascinating character and with whom it's great fun to share a mug, or ten. Apart from the inconvenience of having to repurchase his crockery, given that he never uses the same glass twice, he has many stories that he delights in telling, enjoys a good drink and almost always buys his round. But don't expect to come away with a girlfriend's telephone number on the night Thor accompanies you. You won't exist next to him. It must be his hair as golden as the fields of Asgard, or perhaps his pecs of steel. In other words, the kind of trivial, superficial assets that you and I both know aren't REALLY important, are they? Another guy who knows how to tell stories is John. John Constantine, whom we met in the pages of Alan Moore's *The Saga of the Swamp Thing*, then in the series later dedicated to him, *Hellblazer*. He knows a lot of stories, especially about demons, but these are usually his best ones, rich as they are in vicious details, curvaceous girls and acts whose violence is matched only by their entertainment value. More than anyone else, he'll find his place in a dark corner of the local filthy bar, and will know how to give the room a smoky atmosphere, with the cigarettes he smokes non-stop. Perhaps it has to be said that being a sorcerer, a specialist in the occult arts, brings you into contact with the worst that humanity can produce...

I guess this is an understandable reason to resort to self-destruction through cigarettes and whisky.

I'll end on a slightly lighter note, by mentioning my dear friend Scott Pilgrim (from Bryan Lee O'Malley's eponymous series), who's one of those almost ordinary heroes (yes, yes, compared to those I mentioned above, this Canadian is quite ordinary). I wanted to include him in the list because of his unusual battle (against the ex-boyfriends of the girl of his dreams—literally). Without giving away the whole plot, imagine having to face your sweetheart's ex-boyfriends, only to realize that they're not just bad because they're ex-boyfriends, but are in fact absolutely evil! A fight like that for a girl, I personally can't think of a better reason to buy you a drink!

VIDEO GAMES

FINAL FANTASY

It's common knowledge that every alchemist formulates their unique recipe for their individual Elixir. This alchemical solution harnesses the potency and vivacity of Chocobo extract to fortify the Elixir.

Consuming the Elixir might evoke a sensation of warmth and overall well-being. This experience is typical: it restores your health points and primes you for your upcoming adventures.

CHOCOBO ÉLIXIR
Eggnog, rum and speculoos

INGREDIENTS

4 egg yolks
½ cup (100 g) sugar
6 ⅔ tbsp (100 ml) white rum
2 cups (500 ml) milk
1 cinnamon stick
1 vanilla pod
10 tsp (20 g) speculoos powder (p. 181)

EQUIPMENT

Hand blender

Begin by whisking egg yolks with sugar in a mixing bowl. Gradually add rum until the yolks turn white. Set aside in a cool place.

Pour the milk and add the cinnamon into a saucepan. Slice the vanilla pod in half down its length and scrape out the seeds with the tip of a knife. Add them to the milk, along with the emptied pods, to add extra flavor to the mixture. Heat for 10 minutes over a medium heat, but be careful not to bring to the boil.

Remove from the heat and leave to infuse for a few more minutes.

Remove the vanilla pod and cinnamon stick from the saucepan, then mix the infused milk with the yolks and sugar.

Blend using an immersion blender until smooth. Mix the infused milk with the yolks and sugar. Blend using an immersion blender until smooth.

Serve the eggnog in 4 glasses, generously sprinkling each with speculoos powder. Ready to enjoy – omit rum if serving to a child.

FIND THE CHIP!
Ginger beer, white rum and basil

INGREDIENTS
4 basil leaves
Juice of 1 lime
10 tsp (50 ml) white agricultural rum
2 tsp (10 ml) kiwi syrup
10 tbsp (150 ml) ginger beer
2 ice cubes

EQUIPMENT
Shaker

Thinly slice 2 basil leaves.

Place them in a shaker with the lime juice, white rum and kiwi syrup. Add ice cubes and shake briskly for 30 seconds.

Half-fill a tumbler glass with ginger beer.

Pour the filtered liquid of the shaker directly into the glass.

Decorate the glass with the remaining basil leaves.

As a result of being mistreated by her grandmother, Maple, the Magic Shop salesgirl passes on to you the various potion recipes created by the witch Syrup. By the way, you wouldn't happen to have a Lost Wood mushroom, would you?

THE SYRUP WITCH'S POTIONS

RED POTION
Pomegranate juice, vodka and Freixenet

For 1 BOTTLE OR 1 MARTINI GLASS - Preparation: **2 MIN** - LEVEL ✦

INGREDIENTS

4 tbsp (60 ml) pomegranate juice
4 tsp (20 ml) gin (or vodka)
Juice of ½ lime
4 tsp (20 ml) cane sugar syrup
4 tbsp (60 ml) Freixenet
1 tbsp crushed ice

EQUIPMENT

Shaker

This recipe concocts a potion that restores three hearts' worth of health with just a sip.

Combine pomegranate juice, gin, lime juice, cane sugar syrup, and crushed ice in a shaker. Shake vigorously.

Strain the mixture into a martini glass or potion flask, discarding the crushed ice, and top it off with Freixenet. Behold: Syrup's red potion!

RED POTION (VARIANT)
Fruit mocktail

For 4 BOTTLES - Preparation: **5 MIN** - LEVEL ✦

INGREDIENTS

½ cup (100 g) fresh strawberries
⅔ cup (100 g) fresh raspberries
3 ⅓ cups (800 ml) cranberry juice
¾ cup (200 ml) coconut milk
Crushed ice

This recipe concocts a potion that restores three hearts' worth of health with just a sip.

Begin by preparing the fruit. Wash and remove the hulls from the strawberries. Place the fruit, cranberry juice, coconut milk, and crushed ice into a blender. Blend the ingredients vigorously for 3 minutes.

Next, carefully pour the blended mixture into potion bottles, straining out any leftover crushed ice. Behold: Syrup's Red Potion!

GREEN POTION
Spinach and watercress soup

For 4 **BOTTLES** - Preparation: **25 MIN** - Cooking: **15 MIN** - LEVEL ✦ ✦

INGREDIENTS

1 pound (500 g) spinach leaves
2 bunches watercress
½ cup (100 g) butter

4 cups (1 l) chicken stock
1 cup (250 ml) liquid cream
Salt and pepper

EQUIPMENT

Hand blender

This recipe concocts a potion that boosts your magic gauge with just a sip.

Prepare the spinach and watercress by removing the stems from the spinach and rinsing both vegetables. Pat them dry.

In a saucepan, melt butter, then add the spinach and watercress. Season with salt and pepper, and cook over medium heat for 15 minutes. Add chicken stock and cream.

Using a hand blender, blend the mixture for 3 minutes. Adjust seasoning if needed. Behold: Syrup's green potion!

To serve: Serve your potion in soup plates or opt for a flask for the adventurous young Hylian!

BLUE POTION
Inspired by the Blue Lagoon

For 1 **BOTTLE** - Preparation: **5 MIN** - LEVEL ✦ ✦

INGREDIENTS

8 tsp (40 ml) Hpnotiq vodka
(you can replace Hpnotiq with classic vodka)

4 tsp (20 ml) blue curaçao
4 tsp (20 ml) lemon juice

6 ⅔ tbsp (100 ml) lemonade
Crushed ice

Absorbing one bottle will power you up completely! Isn't that great?

Pour vodka, curaçao, lemon juice and crushed ice into a shaker. Shake briskly for 1 minute.

Pour the contents of the shaker into a glass or flask, straining out the crushed ice. Add the lemonade until the glass or flask is completely full. Behold: Syrup's blue potion! (Follow Syrup's example and sell it for 160 rupees, enough to buy arrows!)

Ahoy sailors! We're not going to set off on a raid without a mouthwash, are we? So, listen up, do everything right, and we should have plenty to cheer us up, I'm telling you!

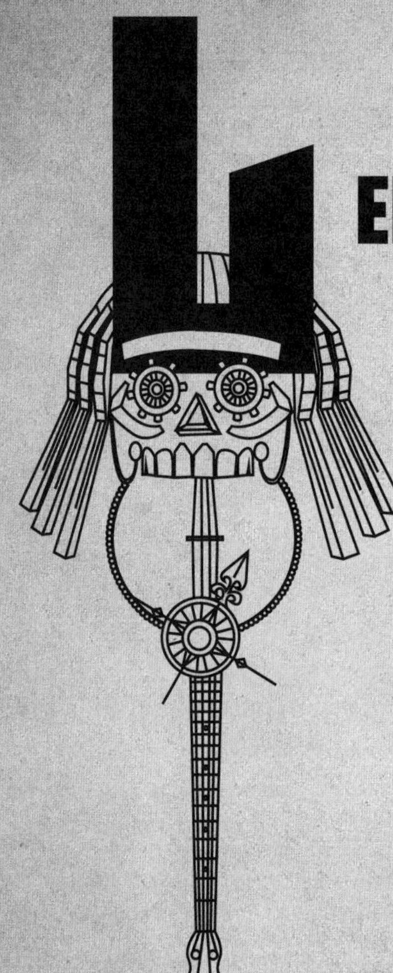

LEMONHEAD
Rum and limoncello

INGREDIENTS

8 tsp (40 ml) Havana Club Gold rum
6 tsp (30 ml) limoncello
10 tbsp (150 ml) Depot sparkling water
2 tsp (10 ml) Kraken Rum
1 twist of lemon

Pour the Havana Club Gold amber rum and limoncello into a mug.

Slowly add sparkling water.

Finally, add the Kraken Rum on top, which will give the mixture a two-tone effect, then garnish with a twist of lemon.

For **1 GLASS** - Preparation: **5 MIN** - LEVEL ✦

As you tackle the circuit, keep centered, apply brakes periodically, and outpace Bowser – his goal is to edge you out. Follow these tips for victory! Oh, and sip on this homemade elixir, it'll keep your focus on the track!

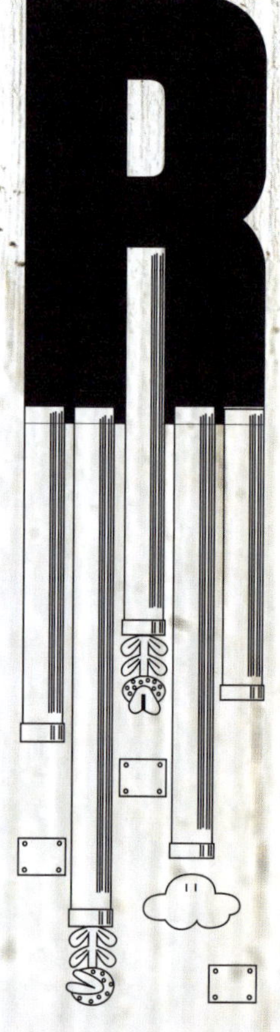

RAINBOW ROAD
Vodka, peach liqueur and rainbow ice cubes

INGREDIENTS

For **1 LONG-DRINK GLASS**
2 red ice cubes (p. 179)
2 yellow ice cubes (p. 179)
2 green ice cubes (p. 179)
2 blue ice cubes (p. 179)

8 tsp (40 ml) vodka
4 tsp (20 ml) peach liqueur
1 bottle Ginger Beer
2 drops Peychaud's bitter

Layer the ice cubes in this order: red, yellow, green, and blue in a glass.

Pour vodka and peach liqueur over them.

Top up the glass with ginger beer and finish by adding the bitter.

CHOCOLATE ISLAND
Cocoa gin, Frangelico and crème de cacao

INGREDIENTS

For **1 TUMBLER GLASS**
8 tsp (40 ml) Cocoa gin
4 tsp (20 ml) Frangelico
4 tsp (20 ml) dark crème de cacao

8 tsp (40 ml) semi-skimmed milk
1 scoop chocolate ice cream
1 square of chocolate
Crushed ice

EQUIPMENT

Blender

For this recipe, there's no need to take the mushroom: With this potion, the stars will be all yours! Pour all the ingredients except the chocolate square into the blender and blend for 2 minutes until you obtain a fine emulsion.

Pour into a glass, garnish with the chocolate square and HERE WE GO!

For 1 BALLOON GLASS - Preparation: **5 MIN** - LEVEL ✦

P OKÉTAIL
Infused gin, wild strawberries and campari

INGREDIENTS

8 tsp (40 ml) Bombay Sapphire gin infused with wild berries
4 tsp (20 ml) Cocchi Rosa Americano
4 tsp (20 ml) wild strawberry cream
4 tsp (20 ml) fresh egg white
2 tsp (10 ml) Campari
Crushed ice

EQUIPMENT

Shaker

That's the kind of drink you won't find at Pallet Town! Put your balloon glass in the freezer so you can serve your Pokétail chilled.

Combine all ingredients except crushed ice in a shaker. Shake briskly for about 30 seconds first (without ice). This dry-shaking will emulsify everything, including the fresh egg white.

Add crushed ice to the shaker and shake again.

Remove the glass from the freezer and strain the contents of the shaker into it.

For a fun presentation, use fruit or chocolate cream to create a Pokéball shape.

For 4 GLASSES - Preparation: 5 MIN - LEVEL ✦

*After escaping from the dungeons and crossing the palace's endless corridors of pitfalls
and death traps, you finally rescued the princess. You even succeeded in slaying the
infamous Jaffar, the vizier, who wanted to destroy you. Would you care for a sweet treat?*

JAFFAR'S DELIGHT
Mint Doogh

INGREDIENTS

1 cup (250 ml) yogurt (p. 179)
2 cups (500 ml) sparkling water
1 tsp mint syrup
1 tsp rose water
A few fresh mint leaves

In a mixing bowl, blend all ingredients except mint leaves until smooth.

Chop a few fresh mint leaves.

Pour the mixture into 4 tall glasses and place the chopped mint leaves on top of
the Doogh foam. Sip through a straw.

DONKEY KONG

GOLDEN BANANA
Banana, Koko Kanu rum and white cocoa

INGREDIENTS

1 banana
1 small red pepper
8 tsp (40 ml) Koko Kanu rum
4 tsp (20 ml) white crème de cacao
2 cocktail spoon vanilla ice cream
1 tbsp crushed ice

EQUIPMENT

Blender

Peel the banana. Cut into thirds.

Cut ⅓ into large cubes. Use a skewer to prick them with the chilli pepper. Reserve the decoration for the rest of the party...

Coarsely chop the remaining ⅔ and place in a blender.

Add the Koko Rum, white crème de cacao, vanilla ice cream and crushed ice, then blend to a thick mousse.

Pour the mixture into the pilsner glass. Place your banana-chilli skewer on the glass.

For 1 BALLOON GLASS - Preparation: 10 MIN - LEVEL ✦

Relax: You've only got a few minutes before your customer makes his appearance in this glamorous salon. Don't reveal your presence by acting too hastily. Give yourself a break and take a few moments to prepare that Florentine decoction you love so much.

REQUIESCAT IN PACE
Amaretto, Aperol and gin

INGREDIENTS
4 tsp (20 ml) amaretto
4 tsp (20 ml) Aperol
8 tsp (40 ml) VII Hills gin
2 ice cubes

EQUIPMENT
Shaker
Cocktail spoon

Pour the amaretto and Aperol into a shaker. Add the ice cubes and shake briskly for a few moments.

While straining the ice cubes, pour the contents of the shaker into a balloon.

Using a cocktail spoon, pour the gin over the mixture to create a separation between the spirits.

There you go... enjoy in peace... until your target arrives...

VIDEO GAMES
Lexicon

A

AMARETTO
Italian almond-based liqueur.

APEROL
Low-alcohol Italian bitter.

B

BLANCHING
Removing the skin from a fruit after plunging it into boiling water for a few seconds.

F

MAKING YOUR OWN FLAVORED SPIRITS
There's nothing like making your own concoctions! Here are a few examples of flavored alcohols that are easy to make at home.

GINGER FLAVORED RUM
INGREDIENTS
2 cups (200 g) fresh ginger
1 ½ tbsp (20 g) brown sugar
3 cups (750 ml) white rum

Peel the ginger and cut into thick sticks. Place them in the bottom of a bottle. Add the brown sugar and pour in the white rum. Leave to macerate for 4 weeks before tasting.

STRAWBERRY FLAVORED RUM
INGREDIENTS
1 ¼ cup (250 g) gariguette strawberries
1 ½ tbsp (20 g) brown sugar
3 cups (750 ml) white rum

Hull the strawberries, then slice them in half. Place them in the bottom of a bottle and add the brown sugar. Fill the bottle with white rum. Leave to macerate for 8 weeks before tasting.

MINT FLAVORED VODKA
INGREDIENTS
1 sprig mint
3 cups (750 ml) vodka

Place the mint sprig in a bottle. Add the vodka and seal tightly. Leave to macerate for 3 weeks before tasting.

CHILI FLAVORED VODKA
INGREDIENTS
3 red peppers
½ cup (100 ml) cane sugar
2 ½ cups (600 ml) vodka

Place the 3 peppers in a bottle. Add the cane sugar, then the vodka. Close tightly. Leave to macerate for 1 week to 10 days before serving.

FRANGELICO
Italian hazelnut-based liqueur.

S

SHAKER
Bar equipment used to mix liquids.

There are 3 types of shaker:

• The Boston shaker: composed of a metal upper part, called the "timbale", and a glass lower part. The diameter of the timbale is larger than that of the glass, so that it can fit inside. The cold action of shaking ice cubes, for example, causes the metal to shrink, ensuring a hermetic seal between the two parts. The Boston shaker's thick glass is designed to withstand thermal shock.

• The continental shaker: made up of 2 parts, a high and a low timbale, all in metal.

• The 3-piece shaker: a classic shaker with a stopper for the timbale and a filter. There's no need to use a strainer, for example, to filter a preparation with this type of shaker; in fact, you can pour the cocktail made in the shaker directly without opening it, just by uncorking it.

A few simple tips for the shaker:

• Never mix fizzy drinks in the shaker, as you could create quite a reaction when you open it (and you don't want that).

• If you're serving a British spy, remember that his vodka martini is made with a shaker, not a mixing spoon.

Tips

MAKING YOUR OWN YOGURT

Yogurt is made by mixing whole milk with lactic ferments. It's the ferments that set the milk and harden the mixture. Whether you buy ferment or store-bought yogurt, remember that it's the quality of the ferment and the milk that will give homemade yogurt its taste and consistency.

As with all good preparations, potions, ointments and milk preparations, the key to this recipe is patience.

INGREDIENTS FOR 1 L HOMEMADE YOGURT
4 cups (1 l) whole milk
½ store-bought yogurt or 1 sachet of ferments from a pharmacy
Ice cubes (if necessary)

• Preheat oven to 45°C (gas mark 1-2).

• Bring the milk to 98°C in a saucepan. Check the temperature with a kitchen thermometer.

• Remove the saucepan from the heat and add either the store-bought half-yogurt or the ferments. Whisk the mixture thoroughly. Allow to cool to 45°C. Place the container on a bed of ice cubes to accelerate cooling if necessary.

• Once cooled to 45°C, pour the yogurt mixture into glass or earthenware pots. Place them in a casserole or large dish and bake for 6 hours. Check the oven temperature carefully, using a kitchen thermometer.

• After 6 hours, remove the jars from the oven and leave to cool to room temperature, then refrigerate overnight before use. And there you have it: homemade yogurt!

TIPS

For vanilla yogurts, infuse an open vanilla pod into the warmed milk, before adding the ferments or yogurt. // For goat's milk yogurts, replace the milk with goat's milk, and the yogurt with goat's milk yogurt. // Your yogurts will keep for almost 15 days in the fridge. You can use one of your own yogurts to make new ones.

MAKING COLORED ICE CUBES

To make colored ice cubes, here are two simple techniques:

• Food coloring

Fill several glasses with clear water. Add a few drops of food coloring—1 color per glass, of course. Pour the contents of the glasses into the compartments of an ice cube tray and freeze for a few hours.

• Syrups: the example of grenadine syrup

Pour 2 dashes of grenadine syrup into an ice-cube mould and add water. Stir with the tip of a knife or the handle of a spoon and set in the freezer for a few hours.

MAKING FRUIT ICE CUBES

You can not only color ice cubes, but also flavor them with fresh fruit, peel, zest, fruit pulp and so on.

Nothing could be simpler: place fresh fruit—raspberries, for example—in each compartment of an ice cube tray and fill with water. Set in the freezer for a few hours.

Sauces

A few homemade preparations of great classics

KETCHUP

INGREDIENTS FOR 4 PEOPLE
1 garlic clove
1 red onion
6 ripe tomatoes
2 tbsp olive oil
2 pinches ground cumin
2 pinches ground ginger
2 tbsp tomato paste
1 ½ tbsp (20 g) brown sugar
6 ⅔ tbsp (100 ml) red wine vinegar
Salt and freshly ground pepper

• Prepare the vegetables: peel the garlic and onion. Chop finely and set aside.

• Peel the tomatoes and cut into large chunks. Set aside.

• Heat the olive oil in a saucepan over medium heat. Add the garlic and onion and sauté for 3 minutes. Sprinkle with cumin and ground ginger and stir in the tomato paste.

• Using a wooden spoon, mix well and add the crushed tomatoes. Stir and add the brown sugar. Bring to the boil, then simmer over a low heat, covered, for 15 minutes, then uncovered for a further 10 minutes, until the mixture reduces. Add the wine vinegar, salt and pepper.

• Finally, using a hand blender, blend the mixture for 2 minutes and strain through a sieve. Leave to cool.

MAYONNAISE

INGREDIENTS FOR 4 PEOPLE
3 egg yolks
2 tsp mustard
2 ½ cups (600 ml) sunflower oil
Salt and freshly ground pepper

All ingredients must be at room temperature, or at least at the same temperature, for cold emulsification to take place.

• Pour the egg yolks into a mixing bowl. Add the mustard, salt and pepper. Using a whisk, blend the ingredients until smooth.

• Drizzle in the sunflower oil evenly, while whisking to build up the mayonnaise.

TARTAR SAUCE

INGREDIENTS FOR 4 PEOPLE
1 onion
2 tbsp capers
6 gherkins
¼ bunch parsley
¼ bunch tarragon
A few sprigs of chives
2 ½ cups (600 ml) homemade mayonnaise

• Prepare your vegetables and herbs: Peel and dice the onion. Set aside.

• Place the capers and gherkins in a blender and chop finely. Set aside.

• Chop the herbs.

• Finally, pour the mayonnaise into a mixing bowl. Add the onion, capers, chopped gherkins and herbs, then whisk to combine.

CAESAR SAUCE (FROM CHEF JEAN-FRANÇOIS PIÈGE'S RECIPE)

INGREDIENTS FOR 6 PEOPLE
6 ¾ tbsp (35 g) grated Parmesan cheese
1 garlic clove
1 ½ tbsp (20 g) anchovy paste
1 hard-boiled egg
1 egg yolk
2 tsp sherry vinegar
Juice of ½ lemon
4 ⅔ tbsp (70 ml) grapeseed oil
10 tsp (50 ml) liquid cream
A few drops of Worcestershire sauce
A few drops of Tabasco

• Using a blender, vigorously blend the Parmesan, garlic, anchovy paste, hard-boiled egg and egg yolk until the mixture is well combined.

• Add the sherry vinegar and lemon juice, then blend for a further 5 minutes.

• While blending at slow speed, add the grapeseed oil, then, when the sauce begins to set, add the liquid cream, Worcestershire sauce and Tabasco to taste and blend until fully incorporated.

BÉCHAMEL SAUCE

INGREDIENTS FOR 1 L SAUCE
5 tbsp (70 g) butter
½ cup (70 g) flour
4 cups (1 l) milk
A few grams of grated nutmeg

• Prepare a roux: Melt the butter in a saucepan and stir in the flour. Whisk to combine, then, off the heat, pour the milk all at once over the mixture.

• Still off the heat, stir and whisk until smooth. Return the pan to medium heat and stir continuously until the mixture thickens.

• Then add the nutmeg and stir.

GENOESE PESTO

INGREDIENTS FOR 6 PEOPLE
1 garlic clove
1 pinch coarse salt
⅓ cup (50 g) pine nuts
1 bunch basil
½ cups (50 g) grated Parmesan cheese
6 ⅔ tbsp (100 ml) olive oil

•Using a pestle and mortar, crush the garlic and coarse salt together. Then add the pine nuts and basil leaves and crush again.

• Once a thick, irregular paste has been obtained, add the Parmesan and olive oil. Mix again to incorporate all the ingredients.

• Tip: you can leave the pesto alla genoese thick or make it more liquid by increasing the amount of olive oil.

MAKING YOUR OWN SPECULOOS DOUGH AND POWDER

To make a fine speculoos powder that will add flavor and texture to your preparations, nothing could be simpler: Crush your speculoos cookies and blend the pieces in a blender until you obtain a fine powder.

INGREDIENTS FOR 1 CUP (250 ML) OF SPREAD
2 ⅓ cups (200 g) speculoos cookies
1 cup (250 ml) sugar-free condensed semi-skimmed milk
1 tsp honey
1 tsp cinnamon

• Using a hand blender, start to grind the speculoos cookies into powder in a mixing bowl, then set the powder aside for a few moments.

• Heat the condensed milk, honey and cinnamon in a saucepan over medium heat. Stir well to blend the ingredients evenly, then pour the still-warm mixture into the soufflé dish filled with speculoos powder.

• Using a spatula or wooden spoon, stir until smooth. Pour into a glass jar and voilà, your homemade speculoos spread is ready!

EQUIVALENTS

VOLUME / WEIGHT

VOLUME	WEIGHT
1 ml	1 g
10 ml	10 g
100 ml	100 g
1 l	1000 g

SPOON / WEIGHT

INGREDIENT	TEASPOON	TABLESPOON
Powdered sugar	5 g	15 g
Flour, semolina	4 g	12 g
Butter	5 g	15 g
Fresh cream	5 ml	15 ml
Oil	5 ml	15 ml
Salt	5 g	15 g
Pepper	2 g	5 g

FOOD / WEIGHT

INGREDIENT	WEIGHT
1 knob of butter	5 g
1 pinch of salt	1 g
1 egg	55 g
1 onion	60 g
1 tomato	60 g
1 potato	100 g

Dear reader,

Video games are imaginary worlds that I particularly enjoy visiting. They're often colorful, sometimes improbable, but their main advantage is that you can't die in them. At least not really, and not permanently, and what bothers me, personally, about death is how mercilessly permanent it is.

In the pantheon of "video game" heroes, Mario undoubtedly sits at the top. A modest carpenter conceived by Shigeru Miyamoto in 1981, he soon becomes a plumber and starts eating a lot of mushrooms, which just goes to show how difficult a career change can be. That said, he teaches us that life lies in green mushrooms and gold coins. Far be it from me to judge this turtle exterminator, for whom the pillars of existence are hallucinogenic substances and money, but I've been happy to do without these lives since I left my teens. The awakenings are too unreliable.

The other major figure in this universe is none other than Link, hero of *The Legend of Zelda* series of games, named after the princess whose CV can almost certainly be summed up in the list of places where she was able to take captive, if you believe that princesses only serve to fill prisons and keep glory-hungry farmers busy. But never mind. For Link, life is a sum of hearts, emptied as they are wounded. Note the poetry! Remembering the adventures I had with him in Hyrule always brings to mind those fairies with their healing powers and the red potions, so tasty and regenerative. I don't know if dear Link sees things the same way: For me, the look on his face when he mentions them and his almost permanent silence are the unmistakable symptoms of a serious addiction. I've tried to dissuade him from continuing to associate with these "fairies", but he lives in denial.

Once Mario's formidable nemesis, Donkey Kong eventually gave up his dead-end career as a kidnapper (leaving that to a far more motivated Bowser) to chase his banana stock. I once tried to ask him about his outlook on life, but he could only answer with grunts, brutal jumps and violent blows to his chest. How a primate can wear an elegant tie but be unable to hold an intelligible conversation is beyond me.

Since I'm talking to you, dear reader, about constructive and respectable activities, I can't resist digressing for a moment to mention the heroes of *Pokémon* (a video game released by Nintendo in 1996), whose lives are summed up by capturing animals—which we'd classify as a relatively fantastic bestiary—as innocent as they are adorable, in order to cruelly throw them into a capsule far too small for them (no doubt to irritate them and exacerbate their combativeness), then launch them into a battle of unparalleled violence. As most of these heroes are children, I've long wondered about this universe, which lacks any ban on child labor or animal protection laws.

But there are others for whom life is hard. Take the inhabitant of Shelter 13, for example; straight out of *Fallout*, this guy grew up in a comfortable shelter, while outside an atomic war was devastating the planet's surface. And then, one fine day, he's asked, with a gentle kick up the backside to push him out the door, to roam this desolate, hostile world in search of a chip to repair the shelter's water filter system.

Put yourself in his shoes. I bumped into this guy shortly after leaving Shelter 13, and in the face of his desperation and dry lips, I handed over my water bottle. He forced me to accept a few "Nuka-Cola" capsules in exchange. I still don't know what I could have done with them. In any case, the poor boy had understood what survival was all about. I saw him again a little later, seasoned and jaded, getting drunk on the local alcohol, the origin of which I'd rather not know. Life can have that effect on men. Life in a desert populated by mutants, certainly.

After this little sojourn in a post-apocalyptic universe, I needed something a little wackier. The island of Melée is my favorite destination for this. This island is one of the settings for the *Monkey Island* series, the first of which was produced by LucasArts and released in 1990. It follows the adventures of Guybrush Threepwood, whose name alone makes pirates giggle and Scrabble players fantasize. This would-be pirate travels the seas solving puzzles and battling real pirates. I'm very fond of this universe, but against all odds, given the pirates' proud reputation as drinkers (which is probably the only thing they haven't stolen), it's not a very good one. Indeed, the beverages found here are mainly used to melt mugs or give texture to your spit. Avoid drinking the local grog at all costs. Unless you've decided to end your life as a pirate. With life at all, in fact.

Among the other universes I've been lucky enough to visit, there's the fabulous world of *Prince of Persia*, whose first adventures created by Brøderbund in 1989 already demanded skill and agility. And then there's *Assassin's Creed*, Ubisoft's famous series featuring assassins, templars and bundles of straw. I never quite understood where everyone got the ability to leap from roof to roof without ever crashing to the ground.

Last but not least, *Final Fantasy*, a video game monument spanning more than a dozen volumes, of which I invite you to particularly remember the 7th, where I myself was able to travel from dodgy bar to family tavern on the back of a Chocobo (golden, please). All these references are part of my warm recommendations for your next travels!

Dear reader, as the pages fly by, I forget to tell you the absolutely fabulous details of my first trip. This story is sure to interest you. After all, you don't yet know anything about the curious artifact my companion bequeathed to me, nor do you know anything about him (or what became of him). Many things happened on one of my most recent journeys, very similar to the first one I made with him. Reading such an account would undoubtedly answer most of your questions (though it would pose even more), and you'd learn many details about universe travel, its secrets and the lessons I've learned from it (which might be useful even to those who are content to survey the territories of a single universe, their own). To tell you the truth, dear reader, I think this story will take some time to tell. But keep your eyes peeled, because, one way or another, I'll tell it to you, in this World or another...

INGREDIENTS INDEX

151 Proof Rum - 20

A

Absinthe - 35, 38
Absolut Vodka Pepper - 136
Agar-agar - 43, 131
Agave syrup - 51, 147
Agricultural Rum - 90, 161
Almond milk - 36
Amaretto - 177, 178
Amber beer - 63, 136
Anchovy paste - 180
Angustora Bitter - 86, 96, 108
Anisette - 38
Antiqua Formula - 139
Aperol - 177
Apple cider - 58, 134
Aquavit - 139
Asparagus - 57
Aztec Chocolate Bitters by Fee Bothers - 114

B

Bailey's - 103, 122
Bamboo shoots - 79
Banana - 80, 144, 174
Basil - 161, 181
Bissap juice - 48, 69
Bitter Fee Bothers Aztec Chocolate - 114
Blackberries - 52
Bombay Sapphire infused gin - 171
Bouquet garni - 29, 44, 104
Brandy - 35
Bread croutons - 104, 123
Brown sugar - 67, 178, 180
Buffalo Trace White Dog rye whiskey - 118
Butter - 29, 57, 58, 68, 107, 133, 163, 181

C

Campari - 92, 96, 139, 171
Candied cherries - 24
Cane sugar - 20 , 23, 58, 61, 92, 95, 113, 140, 162, 178
Caper - 180
Captain Morgan Spiced - 86
Caramel - 69
Caramel coulis - 69
Cardamom - 54
Cardhu - 63
Carrots - 29, 76, 89, 104
Cartron Whitemint - 82
Celery - 104, 133
Celery root - 29
Champagne - 61
Chantilly cream - 43, 58, 69, 80, 107
Chartreuse - 38, 42
Cherry liqueur - 35
Chives - 133, 180
Chocolate chip cookies - 107
Chocolate ice cream - 24, 168
Cinnamon - 30, 54, 58, 113, 117, 158, 181
Cloves - 29, 54, 67, 117
Coarse salt - 29, 181
Cocchi Rosa Americano - 171
Coconut cream - 144
Coconut milk - 162
Coffee - 118
Cognac - 90, 114, 141
Coriander - 104
Cranberry juice - 162
Crémant - 140
Crème de cassis - 74
Crème de menthe - 111
Cucumber - 149
Cumin - 26, 180
Curaçao (blue) - 20, 32, 82, 128, 141, 163

D

Dark chocolate - 24, 107, 168
Dark crème de cacao - 168
Dashi with dried bonito - 89
Delirium Tremens Beer - 134
Dewar's 12-year-old scotch - 108, 122
Drambuie - 108, 122
Dried kikurage - 89, 96

Rittenhouse 100 proof rye whiskey - 23, 42
Rooibos tea - 64
Rooibos tea liqueur - 83
Rose water - 172
Rosemary - 64

S

Saffron - 104
Salt - 29, 57, 68, 104, 133, 149, 163, 180
Savoy Cabbage - 29
Semi-salted butter - 68
Semi-skimmed condensed milk - 181
Shallot - 29, 104
Sherry vinegar - 149, 180
Slivered almonds - 80, 107
Soy sauce - 79
Sparkling water - 20, 38, 76, 79, 89, 128, 166, 172
Speculoos - 158, 181
Spinach branches - 79, 163
Spring onions - 57, 79, 149
Star anise - 67
Strawberries - 52, 80, 117, 162, 178
Strawberry liqueur - 141
Sugar - 52, 68, 90, 107, 144, 158
Sunflower oil - 180

T

Tabasco - 83, 136, 180
Tarragon - 180
Tequila - 32, 48, 69, 92, 95
Tia Maria - 118
Tomato - 180
Tomato juice - 136
Tonic - 51
Tonkotsu broth - 79, 97
Triple sec - 48, 86, 128, 141
Turmeric - 95
Turnips - 29, 96

U

Udon noodles - 79, 96

V

Vanilla - 114, 158
Vanilla flavored yogurt - 80, 179
Vanilla ice cream - 58, 107, 174
Vanilla sugar - 69
Vodka - 48, 82, 103, 111, 117, 131, 136, 141, 168, 178

W

Wakame - 89
Watercress - 163
Watermelon syrup - 83
Whipped cream - 58
Whipping cream - 24, 57, 104, 133, 149
Whiskey - 20, 42
Whisky - 134, 140
Whisky cream - 63
White crème de cacao - 174
White miso paste - 89
White rum - 48, 82, 158, 178
White wine - 83, 104
Whole milk - 24, 107, 178
Wild strawberry cream - 171
Worcestershire sauce - 180

Y

Yogurt - 172, 179
Yogurt liqueur Bowls - 141
Yuzu - 89, 120

Thanks

Stéphanie Simbo

Thanks to my Power Rangers and my family, who gave me support and a smile when I needed it most. To my two "sons" who never lost faith in me.

Thanks to Thibaud. I can't thank him enough for giving me the opportunity to work on this incredible project. Thanks to Bénédicte Beaujouan and the Bureau des Affaires Graphiques, as well as to Hachette Editions, for making it possible for this project to take shape and exist.

Finally, I dedicate this book to Him. He has supported me, seen me and helped me in my most critical moments, and he has been and will remain my source of inspiration for a long time to come. I thank Him.

Thibaud Villanova

A big thank you to my close friends and family, without whom this project could not exist.

To my wife Bérengère, through your unconditional love, creativity and support, you are my source of energy and willpower. Thank you for being so demanding and so talented.

To Adrien, without your friendship and advice, this project and these books could not be as fantastic as they are in my eyes. To Satoru, what a pleasure it's been to share custody of the Traveller we've created! Thank you for giving him such a soul and personality, and for your wise counsel.

In the difficult months during which I wrote this book, a big thank you to my family, my parents and my sister for allowing me to create and develop my life project. To Polly, for being such a pleasant and creative co-author, welcome to the Gastronogeek family!

Thanks to Bénédicte Beaujouan and the Bureau des Affaires Graphiques, Anne Kalicky from Comptoir Éditorial, Guillaume Czerw, Sophie Dupuis-Gaulier and Ayumi Idda, without whom *Gastronogeek* books could not be what they are!

A big thank you to all my friends, past, present and future, who have helped me and trusted me, thank you for your advice, your tips and your sometimes fabulous gestures of friendship: Sébastien Moricard, Thomas Olivri, Nicolas Beaujouan, Olivier Jalabert and Elsa Sztulcman, Max Bender, Julien Laval, Camille Mollard, Anna Imbert, Dominika Roslon, Krystel Maquet, Philippe Vagner, Jérôme Firon, Aurélie Lebrun, Marie-Charlotte Palot, Marie Pottiez, Laura Cadeddu and all those I won't name here but won't forget.

Thank you Marcus, your support for over a year now and the foreword you wrote for this book are a source of pride for me! Thank you for doing us the honor of accompanying us as we conquer the world with our forks!

Special thanks to our friend Pierre Pevel for turning my little worlds into big fantasy worlds. I always keep our discussions and your advice in a corner of my head (next to a signet ring and a winged cat). Thanks also for lending us this fantastic sword, made by Marc Muscadel of Rêves d'Acier!

Thanks to chef Thierry Marx for being such an enthusiastic sponsor, always ready to listen to this project. Thanks to Jeanne and the Album Comics team, Arno and Claude from Pulp's, the Manga Dori team, rue Keller, Marylis Vallet and Émilie Hurel from Bandai Namco, Din, Nadine LeMoing, Kais and the Ghostbusters France association, to Cécile Sikay for her Cosplay elements for Princesse Mononoké, and to Max Bender and Elsa Sztuclman for lending us the elements we needed to delve a little deeper into each of the universes we've covered in this book.

Thank you to Catherine Saunier-Talec, Anne Vallet and Antoine Béon, Johanna Rodrigue-Faitot and Sophie Perfus-Mousselon, from Hachette, for being such wise editors and advisors, thank you for trusting me when I first walked into your office with this crazy project under my arm, and thank you for trusting me again today.

I'd also like to thank all the people who have shown us their sympathy and support and who, since the project was born over a year ago, have never ceased to ensure that *Gastronogeek* as a whole can flourish. So, thank you to everyone who comes to see us at trade fairs and conventions, who writes to us, who populates our social networks, who follows us and gives us their support. Thank you for believing in us, and know that we'll never let you down.

Finally, Stéphanie and I would like to extend our heartfelt thanks to all the creators who gave birth to these universes, these heroes and these characters, who have inspired us so much and to whom we have humbly paid tribute in this book.

MANAGEMENT: Catherine Saunier-Talec

EDITORIAL MANAGER: Céline Le Lamer

ARTISTIC DIRECTOR: Antoine Béon

EDITING: Anne Vallet

EDITORIAL PACKAGING AND GRAPHIC DESIGN: Le BDAG
www.le-bureau-des-affaires-graphiques.com

LAYOUT: Bérengère Demoncy

EDITORIAL COORDINATION, FOLLOW-UP AND PROOFREADING: Anne Kalicky (Comptoir Éditorial)

PROOFREADING: Clémentine Sanchez

PRODUCTION: Amélie Latsch

Printed in China by LPP
Published by Titan Books, London, in 2024.

TITAN
BOOKS

A division of Titan Publishing Group Ltd
144 Southwark Street
London SE1 0UP
www.titanbooks.com

Find us on Facebook: www.facebook.com/titanbooks
Follow us on X: @TitanBooks

Published by arrangement with Hachette Heroes:
www.hachetteheroes.com

A CIP catalogue record for this title is available from the British Library.
ISBN: 9781835410356
10 9 8 7 6 5 4 3 2 1